PROPHECIES IN THE BOOK OF ESTHER

by

Joseph Good

Prophecies in the Book of Esther

By Joseph Good

ISBN-10: 1983915408

ISBN-13: 978-1983915406

4th Printing, February 2018

Copyright © 1995, 1997, 2009, 2018 – Joseph Good

All rights reserved.

שׁ Hatikva Ministries

PO Box E

Nederland, Texas 77627

(409) 724-7601

WWW.HATIKVA.ORG

Table of Contents

1. The Stage is Set	1
2. The Cast of Characters	9
3. Genealogies	19
4. Then Came Amalek	25
5. Pride and Evil	37
6. Dinner	49
7. Just Desserts	57
8. The 17th Day of Nisan	63
Noah's Ark	64
The Parting of the Red Sea	64
King Hezekiah	66
The Resurrection of Yeshua	68
9. Justice	71
Duplicitous Gog – Then & Now	77
10. Redemption	83
11. The Ten Sons	89
The Vav	89
The Decemviri	96
World War II	103
The Nuremberg Trials	105
Judged, Sealed and Executed	108
The False Messiah and the Ten Leaders	110
Adar 13 – 1000 Years Later – Adar 14	112

12. Purim — 117
Therefore They Called These Days Purim — 118
The Two Reasons the Festival is Called Purim — 124
The Institution of Purim — 125

"For if you remain completely silent at this time, relief and deliverance will arise for the Jews from another place, but you and your father's house will perish. Yet who knows whether you have come to the kingdom for such a time as this?"

                Esther 4:14 NKJ

PROPHECIES IN THE BOOK OF ESTHER

Unless otherwise noted, the bible used for the scriptures referenced is the Jerusalem Bible, electronic version.

We gratefully acknowledge the talents and contributions of Teresa Casalino, and Darren Huckey

Teresa for her dedicated service in editing and formatting this edition, and Darren for the beautiful cover design and graphics contained herein.

PROPHECIES IN THE BOOK OF ESTHER

1. The Stage is Set

The complicated tale of court intrigue as seen in the book of Esther unfolds with righteous precision. As a young maiden acquires the highest position a woman may possess in the realm, an entire race of people is spared certain annihilation. She embodies the dignity and faith of a nation, attributes taught to her by a relative in the court. Her beauty and grace are exceptional, persuading a monarch to redirect his own laws. Her bravery and that of her cousin is remembered annually in the joyous festival of Purim. The spring festivities commemorate the heroes and heroine, the fall of a wicked man, and the redemption of a doomed people. Everyone enjoys the love story of the king and his beautiful bride, and all can recall the heroism of the righteous Mordecai. But what really happened hundreds of years ago in Persia's court? Was it love? Was it the love of beauty? Or was it the divine timing of the highest order?

The festival of Purim, found in the book of Esther, occurs on the 14th of Adar which falls in either February or March on the Roman calendar. Although Purim is not one of the Levitical festivals, it is biblically based and part of the inspired word of G-d. Purim has been celebrated by the Jewish people since the beginning of the Persian period in 400 B.C.E.[1] During Bible times, cities that had a surrounding wall would celebrate a second day, called *Shushan Purim*. During this second day, the 15th of Adar, the Jews commemorated the additional day of victory that they were allowed over their enemies in the Persian capital city of Shushan.

The book of Esther is unique in that it is the only book in the Bible that never mentions The Name of G-d directly in the text.

---

[1] Esther 9.27-28

PROPHECIES IN THE BOOK OF ESTHER

However, His Name is found several times encoded into the text.

The name Esther, אסתר, is derived from the Babylonian name *Istahar* which means 'as beautiful as the moon'. Its Hebrew derivative, vocalized *HaEster*, means 'covering' or 'the covering of G-d's face.'

> **And I will surely hide my face in that day because of all the evils which they shall have done, in that they are turned to other gods:**
>
> **Deuteronomy 31.18**

This is, perhaps, one reason why The Name of G-d is not spelled out in the text of the book. Rashi, a Talmudic scholar of the Eleventh Century, stated that there was a concealment of the divine countenance during the days of Esther. Why would G-d conceal His face from those He loved? The rabbis teach that the Jews assimilated into the surrounding cultures and began to forget and neglect their total dependence upon G-d.[2] This caused the conditions that clouded the Divine Image and allowing the concealment of His countenance. Though concealed, G-d never departed from His children but continued to be with them, even in their captivity. The virtue of Mordecai and Esther showed and caused repentance and the return to G-d among the Jews during which time G-d's presence was again revealed.

Although His countenance was covered, it was later revealed to them again. There are at least four times when the ineffable[3] Name of G-d appears in acrostic form embedded in the text of Esther. This ineffable Name, known as the Tetragrammaton, was pronounced only within the Temple and only within the Inner Courtyard known as the *Azarah*. It was pronounced daily during the *Shacharit* or "Morning Service" by the *kohanim* (priests) who had been selected according to lots designating how they were to serve in that

---

[2] (Rabbi Nosson Scherman, 1981, pp. xv-xxxviii)
[3] The adjective 'ineffable' has two senses – one is defying expression or description and the other is 'too sacred to be uttered."

THE STAGE IS SET

morning's service in specific duties. It was only when the priests were standing upon the twelve steps that led into the Temple building that the priests pronounced His Name when giving the Priestly Blessing.[4] The Name was pronounced on one other occasion by the High Priest of Israel and that was on the Day of Atonement. He would pronounce the Holy Name eight times during these Yom Kippur Services.[5] Each time the Holy Name was fully pronounced, all the people would follow by prostrating themselves and saying "Blessed be the Name of the glory of His kingdom forever and ever."[6] The Hebrew letters

י-ה-ו-ה

are vocalized individually as Yod-Hey-Vav-Hey. In Hebrew texts, whenever the י-ה-ו-ה appears, it is pronounced *Adonai* (L-rd) in order to reserve His Holy Name for use only within the sacred domain of His Temple.[7]

---

[4] Numbers 6.22-26, if the Priestly Blessing was pronounced at any other time, or by Priests other than those selected for duty by lots, or they were not upon the twelve steps, then the term Adonai was used in the place of the Tetragrammaton due to its sanctification. Tamid 7.2
[5] Yoma 3.8; 4.1-2; 6.2
[6] Yoma 6.2
[7] The term *Adonai* is reserved for prayer. In general usage *HaShem,* literally "The Name," is substituted for the Tetragrammaton.

PROPHECIES IN THE BOOK OF ESTHER

The Hebrew letters י-ה-ו-ה (Yod-Hey-Vav-Hey) appear in Esther 1.20 as the first letters of four consecutive words when read backward:

הִיא וְכָל הַנָּשִׁים יִתְּנוּ

...*hi v'chal hanashim yitnu*

...it, and all the women will give.

In Esther 5.4 these letters appear again as the initial letters of four consecutive words when read forward:

יָבוֹא הַמֶּלֶךְ וְהָמָן הַיּוֹם

...*yavo hamelech v'haman hayom*

...and let the king and Haman come today.

Then again, in Esther 5.13, the Tetragrammaton is formed by the final letters of four consecutive words when read backward:

זֶה אֵינֶנּוּ שֹׁוֶה לִי

...*zeh ainenu shoveh li*

...this gives no satisfaction to me.

And once more the Tetragrammaton is seen in Esther 7.7 by the final letter of four consecutive words read forward:

כִּי־כָלְתָה אֵלָיו הָרָעָה

...*ki chaltah ailav haraah*

...that his fate had been determined

The book of Esther gives a vivid description of the triumph of the true Messiah and glimpses into the Kingdom of G-d on earth.

THE STAGE IS SET

The book of Esther is unique as a story of ancient accounts, yet it provides a profound vision of the future. More than any other book of the scriptures, Esther deals with the nature of the False Messiah[8] and his demonic hatred of the Jews.

Many years before the events of this story came to pass, the earthly stage was set and the characters were created. The Babylonian Empire had succumbed to the power of the mighty Persian Empire. Nebuchadnezzar had taken the Jews into Babylon in three stages. Among those taken was Daniel, who later served the Babylonian king and sat at his gate, and Ezekiel, along with many more who would later return to Jerusalem. Jeremiah had prophesied that after 70 years of captivity the Jews would return to rebuild the Temple and Jerusalem. No one knows exactly when the 70 years begins or ends. A prince of Nebuchadnezzar, Belshazzar, provoked G-d by using the sacred vessels from the Temple for indecent purposes.[9] Belshazzar died within hours of mishandling the sacred vessels as Cyrus the Mede conquered Babylon, and thus began the Medio-Persian Empire.

Cyrus is regarded in scripture as a just ruler who beheld the awesome power of G-d and vowed that the Temple in Jerusalem would be restored.[10] His reign was short, however, and his empire passed into the hands of his sons, Cambyses and Smerdis. Most scholars agree Smerdis tried to usurp the throne and was later assassinated by the cohorts of Darius I. Cambyses presumably died in battle against Egypt. By this time the foundation for the Temple had been laid, but work stopped and would not commence for another 20 years.[11]

Before his death, Cyrus began restoring the old Elamite city of Susa. Darius continued the restoration and conducted many affairs of state there. Susa is known in the Bible as Shushan. He enlarged the

---

[8] The False Messiah is also known as the Anti-Christ.
[9] Daniel 5.2-4
[10] Ezra 1.1-4
[11] Ezra 4.4-6

PROPHECIES IN THE BOOK OF ESTHER

empire and began a large building campaign. Darius is regarded historically as a great ruler, and according to tradition is the same Darius in scripture who allowed many Jews, such as Ezra, Zerubbabel, and Yeshua the son of Yehozadak the High Priest, to return to Jerusalem and undertake the task of rebuilding the Temple. The Persian Empire flourished under Darius' regime. He was succeeded by his own son Xerxes, who reigned for twenty years and was succeeded by his own son, Artaxerxes, who commissioned Nehemiah to return for the rebuilding of the walls of Jerusalem.

Tradition holds that the Jews were allowed to return during the reign of Darius, but were called back to Persia during the reign of Ahasuerus. The rabbis teach that Ahasuerus, thought to be Xerxes, disliked the Jews and was afraid of their efforts to rebuild the Temple. While no factual evidence supports this recollection of history, such an interruption of the return of the Jews well justifies the story of Esther "for such a time as this." In other words, Esther's intercession on behalf of the very lives of her people, further allowed them to finish rebuilding the Temple as Cyrus had long ago promised.

It is not known for certain exactly which king Ahasuerus represents, but most theologians' support that he must have been Xerxes. This is concluded by the similarity in descriptions of their reigns. Each had a large banquet with many nobles during their third year as monarch. Each is described as being a ruler of numerous provinces. Although nothing exists in Persian history to substantiate the story of Esther, there is also a lack of evidence to discount it. Moreover, the timing of events in the book of Esther coincides with the timing of recorded history concerning Xerxes. In the third year of his reign, Xerxes began his campaigns with the Greeks which lasted until his seventh year, at which time he returned to Persia in order to develop his kingdom. It is during this same seventh year that Ahasuerus takes Esther as his queen. Most of the historical accounts on Xerxes are in Greek literature, therefore, they may have been skewed as Xerxes led several campaigns against the Greeks and lost. His Persian name was *Khshayarsha* which the Greeks translated Xerxes. There are several similarities between Ahasuerus and

THE STAGE IS SET

Khshayarsha. The Hebrew pronunciation of Ahasuerus is *Achashveyrosh.*

Whatever the plight of the Jews during the reign of Ahasuerus, there were many Jews still captive in Persia. Those taken into captivity from the old Babylonian Empire learned to live new lives as foreigners in yet another country. Everything that developed in the story had already been predestined by a higher authority. The redemptive work had already been provided many years before. The stage had been set, and so the story begins.

PROPHECIES IN THE BOOK OF ESTHER

2. The Cast of Characters

There are several characters that play major roles in the Persian court. Ahasuerus is the king. His beautiful, yet vain queen is Vashti. She is later replaced by Esther, the heroine of the story. Esther is a beautiful Jewess who has been reared in the household of her cousin, Mordecai, a righteous man. Esther saw Mordecai as her loving father and greatly respected his guidance and counsel. The villain of the story is Haman the Agagite, an evil man whose pride seeks the power of the realm.

> And it came to pass in the days of Ahasuerus, this is Ahasuerus who reigned, from Hodu to Kush, over one hundred and twenty seven provinces:
>
> Esther 1.1

Ahasuerus is the king of the Persian Empire and rules over 127 provinces from India to Cush. The Persians, along with the Medes, were the conquerors of the Babylonian Empire which had carried the Jewish people into exile. King Ahasuerus represents the supreme power of the world; he holds life and death in his hands. To be noted, many times in the book of Esther, a reference is made to "the King." Any time this nominative is used without the name Ahasuerus, the verse subtly refers to G-d, the supreme King. Hence, Ahasuerus, although he may have been corrupt and idolatrous, is sometimes seen as a picture of the authority of the Most High, G-d.[1] As the story opens, Ahasuerus shows the splendor and glory of his kingdom to his nobles in a banquet set for 180 days.

---

[1] (Rabbi Nosson Scherman, 1981, pp. xxxvi-xxxviii)

PROPHECIES IN THE BOOK OF ESTHER

> That in those days, when the king Ahasuerus sat on the throne of his kingdom, which was in Shushan the capital: In the third year of his reign, he made a banquet for all his princes and his servants; the power of Persia and Media, the nobles and princes of the provinces, being before him: When he showed the riches of his glorious kingdom and the honor of his excellent majesty many days, one hundred and eighty days: And when these days were fulfilled, the king made a banquet for all the people who were present in Shushan the capital, both to great and small, seven days, in the court of the garden of the king's palace:
>
> Esther 1.2-5

Vashti, his queen, appears in the first chapter of Esther hosting a banquet for the women. When Ahasuerus sends for her, her reaction sets into motion a chain of events that provided the opportunity for the Jews to thwart a powerful enemy.

> Also Vashti the queen made a banquet for the women in the royal palace which belonged to king Ahasuerus: On the seventh day, when the heart of the king was merry with wine, he commanded Mehuman, Biztha, Harbonah, Bigtha, and Abagtha, Zethar, and Carcas, the seven eunuchs who served in the presence of Ahasuerus the king: To bring Vashti the queen before the king with the royal crown, to show the people and the princes her beauty; for she was beautiful to look on: But the queen Vashti refused to come at the king's command by his eunuchs; and the king was very angry, and his anger burned in him:
>
> Esther 1.9-12

Vashti is deposed from her position following her refusal to appear before the king and all his male court. Vashti's refusal to

THE CAST OF CHARACTERS

appear was related to the king's demand that she appear before the court to show her beauty wearing her crown.

The king and his men had been drinking for seven days at this time. According to Jewish tradition, Vashti was to appear before the king wearing only her crown and nothing else.[2] Very likely, Vashti was of noble birth herself,[3] thus securing Ahasuerus' claim to the throne. By virtue of her royal birth, she would certainly have commanded a great amount of respect, veneration and ceremonial formality. According to another tradition, the reason Vashti did not appear before the nobles had nothing to do with modesty.[4] Rather, she was unwilling to be so ignominiously summoned at the king's request. Whatever her reasons were, her refusal paved the way for the plans of G-d to be fulfilled through Esther. Throughout the first 18 verses of the first chapter of Esther, Vashti is referred to as the queen or Queen Vashti. After she incites the king's displeasure she is simply referred to as Vashti. Her royal title has now been removed. Vashti's person may represent those caught in paganism who will wind up rejecting the true King's summons[5] and who will be replaced in the future with the rightful queen and bride of G-d, the

---

[2] Babylonian Talmud, Megillah 12b.

[3] The Midrash conveys that Vashti was the orphaned daughter of Belshazzar; G-d was her help and kept her alive and she was wed to the emperor of Persia and Media, even though she was a Chaldean (=Babylonian) (Esth. Rabbah 3:5). In the midrashic account of these events, on the night that Belshazzar was killed, Cyrus the Persian and Darius the Mede were guests at his table. The candelabrum fell and dashed out Belshazzar's brains. Darius was crowned in his stead and sat in Belshazzar's customary place. The death of Belshazzar caused total pandemonium in the palace. Some killed, while others engaged in looting. Vashti, Belshazzar's daughter, was a young girl. She saw the tumult in the castle and ran among the guests. Thinking that her father was still alive, she mistakenly sat in Darius's lap, in the belief that he was her father. Darius took pity on her and married her to his son Ahasuerus. (Midrash Panim Aherim [ed. Buber], version B, para. 1). (Kadari, 2009)

[4] Ibid.

[5] Luke 14.16-24

PROPHECIES IN THE BOOK OF ESTHER

Jewish people and those joined to her.[6] These plans reveal much of the eschatological blueprint to be fulfilled at the Messiah's coming.

> Then said the king's servants who ministered to him, Let young virgins of good presence be sought for the king: And let the king appoint officials in all the provinces of his kingdom, that they may gather together all the young virgins of good presence to Shushan the capital, to the harem, to the custody of Hege, the king's eunuch, keeper of the women; and let their ointments be given them: And let the girl which pleases the king be queen instead of Vashti; And the matter pleased the king; and he did so:
>
> Esther 2.2-4

The princes of Persia counseled Ahasuerus to depose Vashti. They also advised the King to gather beautiful young virgins from the entire kingdom to the royal harem in order to find a new queen.

> There was a Jewish man in Shushan the capital, and his name was Mordecai, son of Jair, son of Shimei, son of Kish, a Benjamite: Who had been exiled from Jerusalem among the captives exiled with Jeconiah king of Judah, whom Nebuchadnezzar the king of Babylon had exiled: And he brought up Hadassah, that is, Esther, his uncle's daughter; for she had neither father nor mother, and the maid was beautiful and of good presence; and, when her father and her mother died, Mordecai adopted her as a daughter: And when these days were fulfilled, the king made a banquet for all the people who were present in Shushan the capital, both to great and small, seven days, in the court of the garden of the king's palace: There were white, green, and blue, hangings, fastened with cords of fine linen and purple to silver

---

[6] Matthew 22.2-9

THE CAST OF CHARACTERS

> rings and pillars of marble; the beds were of gold and silver, upon a pavement of alabaster, marble, mother of pearl, and precious stones: And they gave them drink in utensils of gold, the utensils being different one the other, and royal wine in abundance, according to the bounty of the king:
>
> Esther 2.5-7

Esther, the young Jewess reared by Mordecai, is also very beautiful. Her Hebrew name, Hadassah, means myrtle, an evergreen tree that produces leaves of a sweet fragrance. The myrtle tree is used in several ceremonies: the Feast of Sukkot (Tabernacles); as a substitute for incense during *Havdalah*[7] when incense fell into disuse; at the marriage ceremony when myrtle and palm decked the home; as a garland or crown for a groom; and during funerals myrtle was spread over the coffin. It has been said that roses and myrtles bloom in paradise and the sanctified in heaven bear the branches of myrtle in their hands. Myrtle is an allusion to the resurrection and eternal life because of its longevity. Myrtle also represents the sweetness of Israel to G-d. In the *Haggadah*,[8] myrtle typifies G-d and is often used as an illustration of the righteous people of Israel. Myrtle is used often in the latter books of the Old Testament in this same illustration. For example, in Zechariah's vision, "The myrtle trees that were in the bottom..." typifies Israel in the depths of exile.[9] In this same light, the rabbis taught that Hananiah, Mishael, and Azariah (Shadrach, Meshach, and Abednego) were as myrtle in the fiery furnace; fragrant, righteous, and filled with life.[10]

> So it came to pass, when the king's command and his decree were heard, and when many girls were gathered together in Shushan the capital, to the

---

[7] This is the service at the conclusion of the Sabbath and Festivals.
[8] A Haggadah is the book that contains the order of the Passover Seder.
[9] Zechariah 1.8-11, (Singer, Isidore, 1907, pp. 136-137, Vol 9) Myrtle in *The Jewish Encyclopedia*.
[10] Ibid.

PROPHECIES IN THE BOOK OF ESTHER

> custody of Hegai, that Esther was brought also to the king's palace, to the custody of Hegai, guardian of the women: And the girl pleased him, and she won his favor; and he quickly gave her her ointments, and her appointed portions, and seven maids, chosen to be to given her, from the king's palace; and he advanced her and her maids to the best place in the harem:
>
> Esther 2.8-9

The question arises as to why a good Jewish girl would aspire to marry a pagan. After all, the Torah forbids intermarriage.[11] The answer is partially seen in the second chapter of Esther, verse eight. Although the King James' translation uses the term, "brought also unto the king's house," most exegeses and dictionaries translate the phrase, "that Esther also was *taken* to the king's palace." It may be then that she was taken against her will and had no choice in the matter; according to the custom of that time, to disobey the king would have meant certain death.

> Esther had not declared her people nor her country; for Mordecai had charged her that she should not tell: And Mordecai walked every day before the court of the harem, to know how Esther was, and what was done to her:
>
> Esther 2.10-11

Mordecai instructed Esther not to reveal to anyone that she is Jewish. Every day Mordecai checked on her to learn about her welfare. However, the hand of G-d was seen on Esther as she found favor with all whom she came into contact.

> And when every maid's turn had come to go in to king Ahasuerus, after she had been twelve months, according to the manner of the women, for so were

---

[11] Genesis 34.8-16; Numbers 36; Deuteronomy 25:5

THE CAST OF CHARACTERS

> the days of their purifications accomplished, namely six months with oil of myrrh, and six months with sweet perfumes, and with other ointments for women: Then thus came every girl to the king; whatever she desired was given her to take with her from the harem to the king's palace: In the evening she went, and on the morning she returned to the second harem, to the custody of Shaashgaz, the king's eunuch, who guarded the concubines; she came to the king no more, unless the king had delighted in her, and she was summoned by name:
>
> Esther 2.12-14

Each woman was given a year's preparation, and then she was presented to the king. After each one's night with Ahasuerus, she was taken to the house of concubines. It was not unusual at that time for kings to have numerous wives and concubines.

It is difficult to imagine how Esther must have felt, knowing that she was forever losing any possibility of marriage and family within her own people. However, as will be revealed later, Esther's sacrifice was not only to spare her life and the lives of her family but also the lives of the entire Jewish race. Her role in saving her people and the future restoration of the Temple encompassed more than either she or Mordecai could understand.

> Now when the turn of Esther, the daughter of Abihail the uncle of Mordecai, who had adopted her as his daughter, came to go to the king, she asked for nothing but what Hegai the king's eunuch, the keeper of the women, advised; And Esther found favor in the sight of all those who looked upon her: So Esther was taken to king Ahasuerus to his royal palace in the tenth month, which is the month Tebeth, in the seventh year of his reign: And the king loved Esther above all the other women, and she found grace and favor in his sight more than all the virgins; so that he set the royal crown upon her head, and made her

queen instead of Vashti: Then the king made a great banquet for all his princes and his servants, it was Esther's feast; and he granted a remission of taxes to the provinces, and gave gifts, according to the state of the king:

Esther 2.15-18

Notice that Esther becomes the king's bride and queen in the seventh year of his reign, another perfect eschatological picture of the Messiah and His bride during the seventh millennium.

Mordecai, who adopted Esther, is a key figure in this chronicle of the past and a picture of the future. He represents the Messiah.

Mordecai's father was among those taken into captivity by Nebuchadnezzar. Not only was Mordecai pious and dutiful toward his cousin, Esther, but he also attained a high position at court, that of administering duties within the king's gate.

And when the virgins were gathered together the second time, then Mordecai sat in the king's gate:

Esther 2.19

"Sitting at the king's gate"[12] is an expression associated with being stationed, in service, at the gate. The gate within the palace structure served as a center of auxiliary buildings and offices. It is possible that Mordecai had the duty of providing protection to the inhabitants of the palace, as well as to the king himself. Most of the Persian kings took an entourage of several hundred or thousands of servants on trips to the other cities of the realm. Many of those who stayed close in service to the king were not only servants but also bodyguards. It is well within reason that Mordecai served as an official of the bodyguard staff. Several Jews had served as advisors or servants to kings. Daniel, for example, sat at the king's gate and

---

[12] Esther 2.19, 21; 5.13

THE CAST OF CHARACTERS

ruled over provinces. Later, Nehemiah was cup-bearer[13] to Artaxerxes, son of Xerxes, and was made satrap[14] of Judea.

> Esther had not yet told her country nor her people; as Mordecai had charged her; for Esther did the command of Mordecai, as when she was brought up with him:
>
> Esther 2.20

Earlier, as Esther was taken to the royal harem, Mordecai had instructed her to remain silent on her nationality. The fact that, even after Esther became queen, she still followed Mordecai's instruction, speaks highly of her nature and righteousness.

> In those days, while Mordecai sat in the king's gate, two of the king's eunuchs, Bigthan and Teresh, of those who guarded the door, were angry, and sought to lay hand on the king Ahasuerus: And the matter was known to Mordecai, who told it to Esther the queen; and Esther informed the king of it in Mordecai's name: And when inquiries were made of the matter, it was found out; therefore they were both hanged on a tree; and it was written in the Book of the Chronicles in the presence of the king:
>
> Esther 2.21-23

By this verse, the true integrity of Mordecai is revealed. He saves the life of Ahasuerus by exposing a plot to murder the king. Esther brings knowledge of the devious plot to Ahasuerus and the event is recorded in the king's records. Although Mordecai is not rewarded immediately, his good deeds are recorded for posterity, a

---

[13] Nehemiah 1.11

[14] Satraps were the governors of the provinces of the ancient Median and Achaemenid Empires and in several of their successors, such as in the Sasanian Empire and the Hellenistic empires. (Satrap, 2017)

PROPHECIES IN THE BOOK OF ESTHER

sign to all that G-d remembers and rewards His people, though sometimes the reward does not come until the time of the greatest need.

The villain, Haman, is first mentioned in the third chapter of Esther. His jealousy and greed provide the conflict in the story. However, a greater plot lies under the surface in the epic of good versus evil.

> After these things king Ahasuerus promoted Haman the son of Hammedatha the Agagite, and advanced him, and set his seat above all the princes who were with him:
>
> Esther 3.1

The scripture above shows that only "after these things," the marriage of Esther to the king and the recording of Mordecai's good deed, was Haman allowed to be promoted to his high position. Esther had been chosen because of her beauty and Mordecai had saved the king from an assassination. Only after this, was Haman who hated Mordecai and the Jews raised above the princes. In this manner, G-d provided the antidote before the poison was administered.

The major characters are described in the first few chapters of the book of Esther. But the ancestral development of these characters is often overlooked. Understanding the ancestry of the major characters provides proof that G-d's redemptive plan was already in motion.

3. Genealogies

> There was a Jewish man in Shushan the capital, and his name was Mordecai, son of Jair, son of Shimei, son of Kish, a Benjamite:
>
> Esther 2.5

It is important to remember that genealogies are listed in scripture for a reason. To truly understand the characters in an eschatological sense, it is necessary to examine their heritage and ancestry. Mordecai the Benjamite is from the family of Kish. This particular family plays a major role earlier in the history of Israel. The first king of Israel was Saul, a son of Kish.

> And there was a man of Benjamin, whose name was Kish, the son of Abiel, the son of Zeror, the son of Bechorath, the son of Aphiah, a Benjamite, a mighty man of valor: And he had a son, whose name was Saul, a young man, and handsome; and there was not among the people of Israel a more handsome person than he; from his shoulders upwards he was higher than any of the people:
>
> 1 Samuel 9.1-2

The fact that Mordecai was a descendant of Saul is important when studied in context with the conflict in the story of Esther. According to scripture, G-d orchestrated history to tell what would happen at the coming of the Messiah and the redemption.

PROPHECIES IN THE BOOK OF ESTHER

> For whatsoever things were written aforetime were written for our learning, that we through patience and comfort of the scriptures might have hope.
>
> Romans 15.4

Saul's reign and fall are a classic example of this. When Saul was anointed king of Israel, about 1050 BCE,[1] he had favor with G-d and was a righteous man. However, Samuel, under G-d's direction, warned the Children of Israel against having a mortal for a king instead of G-d the eternal King.[2] True to the warnings of G-d, Saul soon departed from the desires of G-d to do his own wishes. His downfall began with his battle against the Amalekites, one of Israel's oldest enemies. The Amalekites were an ancient people of the land of Canaan who opposed the Israelites as they came out of Egypt on their way to Mount Sinai.

Because of Amalek's evil, he and his descendants became eternal enemies with Israel. King Saul was instructed to battle against the Amalekites and totally destroys them. At that time, the Amalekites were led by King Agag. However, Saul spared his life following the battle. Saul's act of disobedience and rebellion caused the conflict between Amalek and Israel to continue.

> But Saul and the people spared Agag, and the best of the sheep, and of the oxen, and of the fatlings, and the lambs, and all that was good, and would not completely destroy them; but everything that was despised and worthless, that they destroyed completely:
>
> 1 Samuel 15.9

The Bible does not record where this battle took place only that it occurs in a city of the Amalekites. However, following the battle Saul traveled for an undisclosed period of time.

---

[1] (Walton, 1978, p. 50)
[2] 1 Samuel 8.6-18

GENEALOGIES

> And when Samuel rose early to meet Saul in the morning, it was told Samuel, saying, Saul came to Carmel, and, behold, he set him up a monument, and is gone about, and passed on, and gone down to Gilgal:
>
> 1 Samuel 15.12

It becomes evident to have traveled as much as described would have taken several days. When Samuel caught up to Saul, he completed the job that Saul failed to perform. Samuel had Agag brought before him and slew him. After this, the Bible is silent on Agag and his family until the book of Esther where it is revealed that the arch-enemy of Mordecai is Haman.

> After these things king Ahasuerus promoted Haman the son of Hammedatha the Agagite, and advanced him, and set his seat above all the princes who were with him:
>
> Esther 3.1

Haman is described as an Agagite, one who is descended from the family of Agag. The evil Haman would never have been born had Saul accomplished what G-d had instructed him to do. Saul's failure to wipe out the Amalekites allowed the enemies of Israel to live and the line of Agag to continue.

Once again there is a battle between Saul and Agag. Instead, the players are their descendants, Mordecai and Haman. Haman the Agagite is the enemy instead of his ancestor Agag. Due to Saul's disobedience, the line of Agag the Amalekite survives to continue to terrorize Israel in the days of the Persian Empire. Mordecai, the son of Kish and descendent of Saul, succeeds and overcomes the entire lineage of Agag, and is elevated to the highest position in the empire, second only to the king. Likewise, the Jewish people and all who join with them become the favored sons of the kingdom.

PROPHECIES IN THE BOOK OF ESTHER

In an even greater eschatological sense, Saul is a picture of Adam, the first man, and ruler in the Garden of Eden. Yet Adam and Saul fail to uphold G-d'. In this same light, Mordecai is a picture of the Messiah, the second Adam, who will succeed in overcoming all evil. Agag is a picture of Satan. Agag's descendant, Haman, is a picture of the False Messiah.

> But now is Messiah risen from the dead, and become the firstfruits of them that slept. For since by man came death, by man came also the resurrection of the dead. For as in Adam all die, even so in Messiah shall all be made alive. But every man in his own order: Messiah the firstfruits; afterward they that are Messiah's at his coming. Then cometh the end, when he shall have delivered up the kingdom to G-d, even the Father; when he shall have put down all rule and all authority and power. For he must reign, till he hath put all enemies under his feet. The last enemy that shall be destroyed is death. For he hath put all things under his feet. But when he saith all things are put under him, it is manifest that he is excepted, which did put all things under him. And when all things shall be subdued unto him, then shall the Son also himself be subject unto him that put all things under him, that G-d may be all in all.
>
> 1 Corinthians 15.20-28

> And so it is written, The first man Adam was made a living soul; the last Adam was made a quickening spirit. Howbeit that was not first which is spiritual, but that which is natural; and afterward that which is spiritual. The first man is of the earth, earthy: the second man is the L-rd from heaven. As is the earthy, such are they also that are earthy: and as is the heavenly, such are they also that are heavenly. And as we have borne the image of the earthy, we shall also bear the image of the heavenly.
>
> 1 Corinthians 15.45-49

GENEALOGIES

It is remarkable how G-d retells the same story many times so that those who believe in Him may comprehend the depth of the redemption and of the coming of the Messiah.

> That which has been, is what shall be; and that which has been done is what shall be done; and there is nothing new under the sun:
>
> Ecclesiastes 1.9

In order to understand the rise and fall of Saul, as well as the message of Esther, one must first examine the Amalekites. Scriptural passages are rich in examples of the Messiah and the battle with His arch-enemy, the False Messiah. In fact, the *Midrash* states that G-d proclaims that neither His Name nor His throne can be complete until the seed of Amalek is wiped from the face of the earth.[3]

---

[3] Shocher Tov 9.10

PROPHECIES IN THE BOOK OF ESTHER

4. Then Came Amalek

Amalek, a grandson of Esau, became synonymous with Satan in Rabbinic writings. His unprovoked anger and lack of repentance caused the Amalekites to be eternal enemies with G-d. Each of the enemies of Israel from the Roman emperors to Adolf Hitler through today has been tagged with the spirit of Amalek.[1] Of course, the full embodiment of this spirit is seen in the future False Messiah.

The first reference to Amalek in scripture has a most unusual link to the book of Esther. In fact, the passage is unique in several ways. During the days of Abraham four kings came out of Mesopotamia to attack five kings far to the south in the valley of *Siddim*. In the battle the four kings of Mesopotamia were victorious. The details of the battle are described below. What is unique is the fact that the four kings attacked the land of the Amalekites.

> **And they returned, and came to Ein-Mishpat, which is Kadesh, and struck all the country of the Amalekites, and also the Amorites, who lived in Hazezon-Tamar:**
>
> Genesis 14.7

During the days of Abraham, at the time this event took place, Amalek had not yet been born! Abraham is the father of Isaac, Isaac is the father of Esau, Esau is the father of Eliphaz, and Eliphaz is the father of Amalek, four generations from Abraham. The battle mentioned above precedes the birth of Amalek by over one hundred years. The fact that Amalek is mentioned by name before his birth indicates that he plays a prominent role in the history of the Children

---

[1] (Schochet, 1991, pp. 77-79)

PROPHECIES IN THE BOOK OF ESTHER

of Israel. Only two other Biblical characters are prophesied by name before their births in such a profound manner: Cyrus, who was named in a prophecy of Isaiah, also over one hundred years before he lived; and Agag, prophesied in the book of Numbers several years before he was born. Interestingly enough, all three of these men, Amalek, Cyrus, and Agag have a direct bearing on the book of Esther.

The point that Amalek is mentioned before his birth is only the beginning of the revelation of this amazing prophecy. The word Amalek is spelled עמלק in Hebrew. In Hebrew, the words are read from right to left. The first letter in Amalek is the ע, *Ayin* and the last letter of Amalek is the ק, *Kuf*. Counting from the first letter of Amalekites, הָעֲמָלֵקִי, in Genesis 14.7,[2] through all the Hebrew letters until the last character of Amalek the second time it appears in Genesis 36.12,[3] an amazing tie to Esther is discovered. The number of Hebrew characters between the ע of Amalekites in Genesis 14.7 to the ק in Amalek of Genesis 36.12 is exactly 12,110, which is the number of Hebrew characters in the book of Esther![4]

Each year on the *Shabbat* preceding Purim, the following words are read as part of a special Torah portion in congregations all over the world. The name of this Torah portion is *Zachor*, which means "to remember". That is the first word from this Torah passage that concerns Amalek's battle with Israel as they journeyed to the Mountain of G-d,[5] Mount Sinai.

> Remember what Amalek did to you by the way, when you came forth out of Egypt: How he met you by the way, and struck at your rear, all who were feeble

---

[2] This is the first time Amalekites appears in scripture.
[3] It is in this verse that the genealogy of Amalek is recorded.
[4] (Katz, 1996, p. 136)
[5] Exodus 3.12

THEN CAME AMALEK

behind you, when you were faint and weary; and he did not fear G-d: Therefore it shall be, when the L-rd your G-d has given you rest from all your enemies around, in the land which the L-rd your G-d gives you for an inheritance to possess, that you shall blot out the remembrance of Amalek from under heaven; you shall not forget it:

Deuteronomy 25.17-19

Likewise, every believer is on a journey to the mountain of G-d, and will encounter Satan and his forces along the way. The rabbis also noted this in the book of Esther. The Jews were captives in a foreign land, preparing to return to their own country and rebuild the Holy Temple on the Mountain of G-d in Jerusalem, Mount Moriah. The great conflict in the story of Esther is based upon Haman's contempt for the Jews and his desire to keep them from returning to G-d's Mountain.

This is the reason why, of all the enemies of Israel, the Amalekites are singled out as being the worst. When the Children of Israel accepted the Torah, G-d's commandments, they became a holy nation. The Amalekites attack came against Israel immediately before the multitude's acceptance of G-d's ways, thereby trying to hinder the work of the Almighty. The rabbis teach that the Torah was given in the wilderness, proving that it was given to all mankind.[6] If the Amalekites had succeeded, the entire world would not know the benefits of all scripture.

Over 100 years before the Persian Empire, G-d had prophesied that Cyrus, the conqueror of the Babylonians, would allow the Jews to return to Jerusalem and rebuild the Holy Temple on the Mount of G-d, Mount Moriah.[7] True to this prophecy, Cyrus did allow the Jews to return and begin construction of the Temple.

---

[6] (Hertz D. J., 1984, p. 791)
[7] Isaiah 44.28; 45.1-7

PROPHECIES IN THE BOOK OF ESTHER

And in the first year of Cyrus king of Persia, that the word of the L-rd by the mouth of Jeremiah might be fulfilled, the L-rd stirred up the spirit of Cyrus king of Persia, so that he issued a proclamation throughout all his kingdom, and put it also in writing, saying: Thus says Cyrus king of Persia, The L-rd G-d of heaven has given me all the kingdoms of the earth; and he has charged me to build him an house in Jerusalem, which is in Judah: Who is there among you of all his people? His G-d be with him, and let him go up to Jerusalem, which is in Judah, and build the house of the L-rd G-d of Israel, he is the G-d, which is in Jerusalem: And whoever remains in any place where he sojourns, let the men of his place help him with silver, and with gold, and with goods, and with beasts, beside the freewill offering for the house of G-d which is in Jerusalem:

Ezra 1.1-4

From the fourth chapter of Ezra, it is revealed that enemies within the land tried to discourage the rebuilding of the Temple from the time of Cyrus until Darius. This ploy involves the kings of Persia, Ahasuerus, and Artaxerxes.[8] The ancient sages taught that the evil of Haman was not only his desire to kill the Jews but also was in accord with the ploy to stop the rebuilding of the Temple and stop the Jews from returning home.

The struggle of the Children of Israel with the Amalekites is recorded on numerous occasions. The Amalekites were chief among Israel's enemies and their desire to keep G-d's people from worshipping Him and observing His commandments was their highest priority. Another major passage that deals with Amalek's attack upon Israel as Israel journeyed to Mount Sinai is found in Exodus 17.

---

[8] Ezra 4.6-7

THEN CAME AMALEK

Then came Amalek, and fought with Israel in Rephidim: And Moses said to Joshua, Choose for us men, and go out, fight with Amalek; tomorrow I will stand on the top of the hill with the rod of G-d in my hand: So Joshua did as Moses had said to him, and fought with Amalek; and Moses, Aaron, and Hur went up to the top of the hill: And it came to pass, when Moses held up his hand, that Israel prevailed; and when he let down his hand, Amalek prevailed: But Moses' hands were heavy; and they took a stone, and put it under him, and he sat on it; and Aaron and Hur stayed up his hands, the one on the one side, and the other on the other side; and his hands were steady until the going down of the sun: And Joshua discomfited Amalek and his people with the edge of the sword: And the L-rd said to Moses, Write this for a memorial in a book, and recite it in the ears of Joshua; for I will completely put out the remembrance of Amalek from under heaven: And Moses built an altar, and called its name Adonai-Nissi: For he said, Because the L-rd has sworn that the L-rd will have war with Amalek from generation to generation:

Exodus 17.8-16

Few passages of scripture have received as much comment as this one by the ancient commentators. It is extremely rich in imagery and in messages.

As mentioned before, the Children of Israel were on their way to Mount Sinai when Amalek attacked. Many of the commentaries start with the phrase, "Then came Amalek," making note of the word "Then." Why is this word used? It would seem that the logical way to express this would be, "Amalek came and fought with Israel in *Rephidim*," The answer is found in the word *Rephidim*, which comes from a root word in Hebrew meaning "to be slack or remiss." Indeed,

PROPHECIES IN THE BOOK OF ESTHER

in the preceding verses[9] Israel had been striving with G-d to the point of questioning, "Is the L-rd among us or not?" The rabbis stated that it is this lack of faith in G-d, Who had just recently delivered them from Egypt and destroyed their enemies in the Red Sea that allowed Amalek, a type of Satan, to attack them. When a believer strives with G-d and departs from Him, the enemy has an opening to attack.

After the defeat of Amalek, G-d instructed Moses to "Write this for a memorial in the book and recount it in the hearing of Joshua that I will utterly blot out the remembrance of Amalek under heaven." The term for "memorial" and "remembrance" in Hebrew is *Zikaron*. There is a custom during Purim at the reading of the *Megillah* (the scroll) of Esther, to blot out the name of Haman the Amalekite. This is achieved by booing, shouting, and using noisemakers when Haman is pronounced. It's also customary to write the name of Haman on the bottom of one's shoes with chalk and to "stamp him out" while booing. It is noteworthy that G-d has recorded that He will blot out the name of Amalek and all those who are of his spirit. G-d also records in a Book of Remembrance *(Sefer haZikaron)* those who love Him.

> **Then those who feared the L-rd spoke to one another; and the L-rd listened, and heard it, and a book of remembrance [Sefer haZikkaron] was written before him for those who feared the L-rd, and who took heed of his name:**
>
> Malachi 3.16

There are many Messianic references in this passage, as well as allusions to Satan and his human counterpart, the False Messiah.

Moses built an altar to G-d and named it *Adonai Nissi*, "The L-rd is my Banner." The word *Nissi*, (banner, flag, and ensign) is a term used many times in the scripture for the Messiah. Probably the most profound is from the prophet Isaiah. His eleventh chapter is

---

[9] Exodus 17.1-7

THEN CAME AMALEK

one of the most famous passages in the entire Bible concerning the Messiah.

> And in that day there shall be a root of Jesse, who shall stand for a banner of the people; to it shall the nations seek; and his resting place shall be glorious:
>
> Isaiah 11.10

The day referred to is the Messianic Kingdom or Millennium. At that time the root of Jesse, the Messiah Yeshua, will stand as a *Nissi* to both Jews and non-Jews; and His rest, *M'nuchah* (the Messianic Kingdom), will be glorious. In several other passages from Isaiah, the Messiah is presented as the *Nissi*,[10] in the context of the resurrection, the coming of Elijah, and His return. The implication from Exodus 17 is that when Moses lifted up his hands, with the "rod of G-d," it was as the Messiah being lifted up, Joshua prevailed against Amalek, but when his hands were down (the Messiah not being lifted up) Amalek prevailed.

In Exodus 17.12, Moses began to tire and his hands became heavy; therefore, "Aaron and Hur sat him upon a stone, and put it under him, and he sat thereon." This stone that Moses rested on is a picture of the Messiah. The first example of finding rest on a stone is in Genesis 28, a passage that has affected the Jewish people through the ages. This passage is understood to be very eschatological in its content. Jewish worship of G-d received its structure in Genesis 28. The two sons of Isaac, Jacob and Esau, were each taught the precepts of the faith by their father. Esau, more favored by his father, was irresponsible and departed from G-d becoming undeserving of his inheritance. Jacob fled from his brother Esau and was in essence expelled from the land. In rabbinical literature, Esau, also called Edom, is often seen as a type of Rome[11] who expelled the Jews out of the ancient land of Israel in both 70 CE and 135 CE, Jacob sinned but then repented, meeting G-d in exile

---

[10] Isaiah 13.2-3; Isaiah 18.3; Isaiah 62.10
[11] (Culi, 1979, pp. 277, Vol 1)

PROPHECIES IN THE BOOK OF ESTHER

where he embraced the precepts and the covenant that had been handed down to him through Isaac and Abraham. Therefore, he became deserving of the inheritance promised to his grandfather.

While in flight, Jacob stops for the evening in what is designated in English as "a certain place." In Hebrew, the word for "place" is *Makom,* which is also a Hebraic expression for G-d who is frequently called *haMakom,* or "the Place." So too, a hidden reference to G-d is found using *haMakom* in the book of Esther.[12] The rabbis noted that the first verse in this passage had three references to *haMakom* and so it was recognized as an important passage.

> And he lighted upon a certain place [makom], and tarried there all night, because the sun was set; and he took of the stones of that place [makom], and put them under his head for his pillows, and lay down in that place [makom] to sleep.
>
> Genesis 28.11

In the next verse, Jacob lay down to sleep as the "sun has already set," another picture-type of the Messiah as the sun.[13] Jacob took a stone from that *Makom* and lay down to rest.[14] As he rested, he dreamt and saw the Gate of Heaven, angels ascending and descending upon a ladder reaching from heaven to earth. As Jacob awoke the next morning, he realized how awesome this *Makom* was, making a play on words in Hebrew. He realized that this was the Gate of G-d on Earth and he named the place *Bethel,* the House of G-d. There is a town in both ancient and modern Israel known as Bethel, but this is not the place he was referring to. Rather, it was Mount Moriah in Jerusalem, the site of the future Holy Temple, the House of G-d. Jacob took the stone he used for a pillow and set it up as a memorial. He then took oil and anointed the stone. The word

---

[12] (Sabua, 1992)
[13] Psalm 19.5-6; Malachi 3.20 (4.2)
[14] Rest - *M'Nuchah* - a term used for Messianic Kingdom or Millennium.

THEN CAME AMALEK

that is used for the anointing of the stone is *yatzak*, which literally translates "to pour."[15] This action of pouring oil, symbolic of the Holy Spirit, was how one was anointed for service. The term "the Messiah" comes from the Hebrew word *haMashiach* which means "the anointed one." Just as Jacob anointed the stone, a symbol of the Messiah, so will Israel as a nation accept haMashiach.[16] Jacob returned after 20 years in the "Diaspora" to the inheritance of G-d, as a parallel to Israel returning and becoming a nation after 2,000 years of dispersion.

Throughout the Hebrew Scriptures, the Messiah is frequently referred to as a stone. In Genesis 49, concerning the prophecies of the tribe of Joseph, the Messiah is referred to as "the shepherd, the stone of Israel."[17] Daniel in his second chapter refers to "the stone that was cut out of the mountain without human hands." This stone will fill the entire earth.[18] According to some *Midrashim*, this stone is the Messiah.[19] So we can see why the stone that Moses rested upon is a picture of the Messiah. Clearly, the Messiah is represented in this passage about Amalek.

G-d has declared war on Amalek throughout the generations. This battle, however, is fought in the context of the Messiah through faith.

Another major prophecy concerning Amalek and his destiny is found in Numbers 24. This very profound prophecy of Balaam reveals the final outcome of this ongoing war.

> And when he looked on Amalek, he took up his discourse, and said, Amalek was the first of the nations; but his latter end shall be that of everlasting

---

[15] Genesis 28.18
[16] Romans 11.25; Isaiah 59.20-21; Ezekiel 39.22; Isaiah 10.12, 20-23 (Rosenberg, 1982, pp. 470, 543-544, Vol 2)
[17] Genesis 49.24
[18] Daniel 2.34-35
[19] (Ginzberg, 1987, pp. 72, Vol 6)

PROPHECIES IN THE BOOK OF ESTHER

perdition: And he looked on the Kenites, and took up his discourse, and said, Strong is your dwelling place, and you put your nest in a rock: Nevertheless the Kenite shall be destroyed; Where shall Assyria carry you away captive: And he took up his discourse, and said, Alas, who shall live when G-d does this: And ships shall come from the border of Kittim, and shall afflict Assyria, and shall afflict Eber, and he also shall perish forever:

Numbers 24.20-24

The last days are spoken of as events that will take place during the "Birth Pains of the Messiah," called the Tribulation by some Christians. In the prophecy, Amalek is called the first of the nations, a reference to Amalek being the first to attack Israel. In addition, Amalek was a grandson of Esau, the older of the twins born to Isaac. Isaac's other twin son Jacob became the grandfather of Pharez, *Peretz*,[20] and the ancestor of the Messiah. The same generation that saw Amalek saw Pharez. Then just before this passage speaking of the beginning and end of Amalek, is one of the most profound verses on the coming of Messiah foretelling the star of his birth.[21] Amalek was the first of the nations to make war against Israel, and though he takes many forms throughout the ages, his total destruction will be the final note in the war against Hashem, His Messiah and the nation of Israel.

There is yet more in this same passage concerning the nature of Amalek. Identifying three nations helps in understanding the prophecy and further defining Amalek's character. The first to note is *Asshur*, another spelling for the nation of Assyria, which is a type for Gog and Magog (Russia)[22] in the last days. The second nation to be identified is *Chittim*, also spelled *Kittim*, who was understood to

---

[20] *Peretz* is the Hebrew pronunciation of Pharez, about whom there is much commentary concerning the spelling of his name as he is a prominent ancestor to the Messiah.
[21] Numbers 24.17
[22] (Eisemann, 1977, pp. 579, Vol 2)

THEN CAME AMALEK

be the Romans in ancient times.[23] Finally, *Eber* is understood to be another term for the nation of the Hebrews or Israel. The prophecy relates how Russia will attack Israel in the war of Gog and Magog. Following the defeat of Russia's armies by G-d in Israel, Russia will be attacked by the False Messiah and his revised Roman Empire, Europe, The False Messiah's victorious emergence in the aftermath of this invasion of Russia establishes him as the most powerful ruler in the world. The last phrase in Balaam's prophecy states, "and he also shall perish forever," which is understood to be a reference to Amalek,[24] who is a type of the False Messiah. Further, this identifies Amalek as the evil spirit behind all of the armies against G-d during the Birth Pains.[25]

In an earlier prophecy of Balaam's, there is an interesting reference to Agag, the king of the Amalekites, whom Saul was commanded to destroy.

> He shall pour the water out of his buckets, and his seed shall be in many waters, and his king shall be higher than Agag, and his kingdom shall be exalted:
>
> Numbers 24.7

The last phrase concerns the king from Jacob that will be higher than Agag. He is none other than the Messiah of Israel, and indeed His kingdom shall be exalted. An interesting observation concerning Agag is that Saul was commanded to totally obliterate the Amalekites. Failing to follow through to obliterate every living Amalekite, King Saul puts into the motion the birth of Haman before dying himself at the hand of an Amalekite.[26] Perversely, the goal of Haman the Amalekite was to totally destroy the Children of Israel. In due course, G-d reversed this, and it was the followers of Haman

---

[23] (Etheridge, 2017) Targum Onkelos on Numbers 24.24; Targum Yonathon ben Uzziel on Daniel 11.30
[24] Found in Nachmanides commentary on Numbers 24.24.
[25] For a more in depth look at the Birth Pains, see the author's book "*Rosh HaShanah and the Messianic Kingdom to Come.*"
[26] 2 Samuel 1.8-10

PROPHECIES IN THE BOOK OF ESTHER

who were destroyed in the end.

The Amalekites, descendants of Esau, continue to bear resentment toward the descendants of Jacob. As Esau had tried to keep Jacob from his inheritance, likewise the Amalekites tried to hinder the Children of Israel from receiving the Torah and entering the land promised to them generations before.

5. Pride and Evil

Why did the rabbis state that to study the book of Esther one must first understand the position of Amalek and his destiny? The answer is that the book of Esther is more than a historical account of a struggle between Haman and Mordecai. It is a chronicle of the war that has gone on between G-d and Satan from the beginning of time.

The third chapter of Esther begins with the first introduction of Haman the Agagite when King Ahasuerus promotes him above all the officers of the king.

> And all the king's servants, who were in the king's gate, bowed, and did obeisance to Haman; for the king had so commanded concerning him; But Mordecai did not bow, nor did him obeisance: Then the king's servants, who were in the king's gate, said to Mordecai, Why do you transgress the king's command: Now it came to pass, when they spoke daily to him, and he did not listen to them, that they told Haman, to see whether Mordecai's words would stand; for he had told them that he was a Jew:
>
> Esther 3.2-4

Haman presided in the king's gate, the same gate where Mordecai discharged his duties within the kingdom. King Ahasuerus had commanded at the sight of Haman all subjects were to bow and prostrate before him. Mordecai the Jew refused. A tradition of the ancient rabbis teaches that Haman had an image of an idol attached

PROPHECIES IN THE BOOK OF ESTHER

to his belt.[1] It is definitely within Jewish *Halacha* (Jewish ruling) to bow before an official of the kingdom,[2] but never is it allowed to prostrate oneself before an idolatrous image.

Again, this runs parallel with what the scriptures reveal about the coming False Messiah who will have an image constructed of his own self, requiring all people to bow and worship before it. This image is known as the Abomination of Desolation.[3] Man has an inherent nature to worship, for this reason rulers of kingdoms and empires, almost from the beginning of time, have placed their images on coins and statues.

> And when Haman saw that Mordecai did not bow, nor did him obeisance, then was Haman full of wrath: And he disdained to lay hands on Mordecai alone; for they had told him the people of Mordecai; therefore Haman sought to destroy all the Jews who were throughout the whole kingdom of Ahasuerus, the people of Mordecai:
>
> Esther 3.5-6

The plot of the story thickens as Haman seeks to destroy the Jews. The fact that Mordecai has refused to bow down to him fans Haman's passionate hatred of the Jews. The truth is that Haman was full of pride, and this pride allowed his hatred to extend not only to Mordecai but Mordecai's entire race.

This same pride is the pride described for both Satan and his agent, the False Messiah. Possibly the most famous scriptural passage on the False Messiah is in Revelation 13, where the False Messiah is represented as a seven-headed beast that rises out of the sea.

---

[1] (Zlotowitz, 1976, pp. 64-65)
[2] 2 Samuel 14.22
3 Daniel 9.27, 11.31, 12.11; Matthew 24.15; Mark 13.15; Revelation 13.14-15

PRIDE AND EVIL

> And I stood upon the sand of the sea, and saw a beast rise up out of the sea, having seven heads and ten horns, and upon his horns ten crowns, and upon his heads the name of blasphemy.
>
> Revelation 13.1

To modern readers, this seven-headed beast is unique in the scripture, but in the time of the ancient Jews, he was known as Leviathan, of whom scripture has much to say.

> You parted the sea by your strength; you broke the heads of the crocodiles in the waters: You crushed the heads of Leviathan, and gave him for food to the people inhabiting the wilderness:
>
> Psalm 74.13-1

> Can you draw out Leviathan with a hook? Or press down his tongue with a cord: He beholds all high things; he is a king over all the sons of pride:
>
> Job 40.25b-41.26 (41.1-34)

In other words, Leviathan is a type of the False Messiah. This last verse shows that the followers of the False Messiah are as the children of pride and Leviathan is the king over all of them.

Again, Haman in his pride continues to portray the coming evil king. Haman is certainly not the first whose pride encourages annihilation of the Jewish people. More than likely, his ancestry plays an important part in his hatred of the Jews.

Others whose ambition and pride overtake their reasoning are likewise a picture of pride incarnate as seen in the False Messiah. Absalom is a perfect picture of ambition and pride. Absalom was a son of David who sought to take his father's throne. In his attempt,

PROPHECIES IN THE BOOK OF ESTHER

Absalom sat at the gates to make judgments for the people, eventually persuading them against his father, the king.[4] Absalom was very handsome and greatly loved by David. In fact, his pride and beauty were the cause of his death, showing that the downfall of Satan and his forces are linked to this blinding pride.

This same pride was exhibited by Herod at the time of Yeshua's birth. Herod was a tyrant king whose claim to the throne was shaky. Upon hearing that a ruler had been born who would "shepherd Israel,"[5] he devised a plan to rid himself of this other possible heir to his throne. The tragic events that followed are a result of Herod's command to slay the male children of Bethlehem.[6]

Haman's hatred for Mordecai was directed not only to Mordecai but the entire Jewish race. This is exactly how Satan works, using pride channeled into anti-Semitism expressed in destructive hatred and death. It is at this point that Haman began to plot the destruction of both Mordecai and the Jewish people. In a like manner, Satan has always plotted the destruction of Yeshua as well as the entire race of the Jews.

Haman began his own self-destruction as he planned the destruction of the Jews. This same spirit that led Haman also led Adolf Hitler during World War II as he initiated the holocaust. Hitler actually diverted trains that could have been used to evacuate his retreating troops, or at least kept them supplied with ammunition, in order to carry Hungarian Jews to his death camps. His blind anti-Semitic hatred in large part was responsible for his defeat. So it was with Haman.

> Whoever digs a pit shall fall in it; and whoever rolls a stone, it will return upon him:
>
> Proverbs 26.27

---

[4] 2 Samuel 15.2-6
[5] Matthew 2.6
[6] Matthew 2.16

PRIDE AND EVIL

Here is the old battle between Satan and G-d carried out on the battlefield of the Children of Israel. From the beginning, Satan has tried in vain to carry out this evil plot. First through Pharaoh, destroying all the Israelite newborns in Egypt at the time of Moses, followed centuries later by Antiochus Epiphanies IV who waged war against the Jewish people and their G-d in the second century BCE. This same battle takes place against the Messiah during the time of Herod when the infants of Bethlehem were slain at Herod's command. Each of these men portrays graphic examples of the False Messiah to come. These and Haman were identified by their vanity and pride. The extreme and unreasonable hatred of Haman toward Mordecai and all the Jewish people can only be explained as a demonic, anti-Semitic spirit.

In the following verse from the book of Esther, Haman begins to develop his plans of destruction for the Jews.

> In the first month, that is, the month Nisan, in the twelfth year of king Ahasuerus, they cast Pur, that is, the lot, before Haman from day to day, and from month to month, to the twelfth month, that is, the month Adar:

Esther 3.7

Nisan is the first month on the Religious Calendar of the Jews while Adar is the twelfth month. The fact that Haman had lots cast for the correct time to attack the Jews indicates that he was a man that dealt in the occult. Haman created a total blueprint for destruction before he ever approached King Ahasuerus.

> And Haman said to king Ahasuerus, There is a certain people scattered abroad and dispersed among the people in all the provinces of your kingdom; and their laws are different from those of every other people; and they do not keep the king's laws; therefore it is not for the king's profit to tolerate

PROPHECIES IN THE BOOK OF ESTHER

> them: If it please the king, let it be decreed that they may be destroyed; and I will pay ten thousand talents of silver to the hands of those who have the charge of the business, to bring it into the king's treasuries:
>
> Esther 3.8-9

Notice that his main complaint to the king is that these people are "diverse" or different. Of course, what Haman is referring to is that the Jews keep G-d's Torah. According to Jewish law, only certain foods may be eaten while others are forbidden.[7] Also in accordance with the Torah, Jews dress differently[8] which distinguishes them as a people and may seem peculiar to other races. There are other commandments as well that distinguish the Jews from the other nations of the world. The Jew's devotion to G-d superseded their devotion to an earthly king, and when the commandments of an earthly king contradict the law of G-d, the pious obey G-d. So it was with Mordecai when faced with bowing before Haman and his idolatry as stated earlier. This is the basis upon which Haman tells the king that these people do not keep the king's laws. Haman's hatred for the Jews dictates that he is prepared to pay a personal fortune in order to enjoy their destruction.

> And the king took his ring from his hand, and gave it to Haman the son of Hammedatha the Agagite, the Jews' enemy: And the king said to Haman, The silver is given to you, the people also, to do with them as it seems good to you: Then were the king's scribes called on the thirteenth day of the first month, and there was written according to all that Haman had commanded to the king's satraps, and to the governors that were over every province, and to the rulers of every people of every province according to

---

[7] Leviticus 11
[8] Leviticus 19.19; Numbers 15.38-40

PRIDE AND EVIL

its writing, and to every people in their own language; in the name of king Ahasuerus was it written, and sealed with the king's ring:

Esther 3.10-12

The course is now set, the Jews are to be destroyed 11 months later on the 13th of Adar. According to the law of the Persians, the signet from the ring of a Persian king, once applied to an edict, cannot be revoked.

Then were the king's scribes called on the thirteenth day of the first month, and there was written according to all that Haman had commanded to the king's satraps, and to the governors that were over every province, and to the rulers of every people of every province according to its writing, and to every people in their own language; in the name of king Ahasuerus was it written, and sealed with the king's ring: And the letters were sent by couriers to all the king's provinces, to destroy, to kill, and to annihilate all Jews, both young and old, little children and women, in one day, on the thirteenth day of the twelfth month, which is the month Adar, and to plunder their goods: The copy of the decree was given out as a law in every province, to be proclaimed to all the peoples, so that they should be ready for that day: The couriers hurried out by the king's command, and the decree was given in Shushan the capital; And the king and Haman sat down to drink; but the city Shushan was in consternation:

Esther 3.12-15

It may be said that whoever moves against Israel finds he is fighting against G-d. The day Haman approaches the King is on the 13th day of the month Nisan. Although the book of Esther does not elaborate, by the date over which the events just transpired, and those about to occur, all take place within the season of Passover.

PROPHECIES IN THE BOOK OF ESTHER

Moreover, the following verse identifies the twelfth month as Adar, the month that precedes Nisan on the Jewish calendar.

> And Mordecai told him of all that had happened to him, and of the sum of money that Haman had promised to pay to the king's treasuries for destroying the Jews: Also he gave him the copy of the written decree that was issued at Shushan to destroy them, to show it to Esther, and to declare it to her, and to charge her that she should go to the king, to make supplication to him, and entreat him for her people: And Hatach came and told Esther the words of Mordecai:

Esther 4.7-9

On this same day, the 13th of Nisan, Mordecai goes to Esther and tells her of the plot, imploring her to use her position to intercede for the Jewish people. The problem is that the queen is only allowed an audience with the king at his summons. The penalty for approaching the king without his summons is death unless the king extends his golden scepter, thereby granting the gift of life.

> Again Esther spoke to Hatach, and gave him a command for Mordecai: All the king's servants, and the people of the king's provinces, know, that whoever, whether man or woman, shall come to the king into the inner court, who is not called, there is a law; to put him to death, except such to whom the king shall hold out the golden scepter, that he may live; but I have not been called to come to the king these thirty days:

Esther 4.10-11

It is interesting that Esther, in approaching the throne of the king, is guilty of a crime against the king of all the earth with the penalty of death. Only by the grace given to her by the king as he extends his scepter is she granted life. The Hebrew word for "scepter" in this verse is *Sharvit*, which was used in the later periods

PRIDE AND EVIL

of biblical Hebrew. The word used in earlier times was *Shevet*. The *Shevet*, or scepter, was established from the ancient times as speaking of the Messiah. We see in the prophecy given by Jacob that the scepter is referring to the Messiah.

> The staff shall not depart from Judah, nor the scepter from between his feet, until Shiloh come; and to him shall the obedience of the people be:
>
> Genesis 49.10

Another prophecy from the Torah that defines the scepter as being the Messiah is seen in the prophecy of Balaam.

> I shall see him, but not now; I shall behold him, but not near; there shall come a star out of Jacob, and a scepter shall rise out of Israel, and shall strike the corners of Moab, and destroy all the sons of Seth:
>
> Numbers 24.17

In the Aramaic paraphrase of the Torah known as the *Targum Onkelos*, this verse definitely shows the *Shevet* as the Messiah. The *Targum* reads: "Kings shall arise out of Jacob, and the Messiah will be anointed from Israel, and reign over all nations." Notice that the Scepter, or *Shevet*, from the scripture, has become the Messiah in the paraphrase.

Another passage from the ancient Jewish writings that illustrate the Scepter as being a picture of the Messiah is found in the book of Third Enoch, a part of the Pseudepigrapha.[9]

> When the Holy One, blessed be he, sits on the throne of judgment, Justice stands on his right hand, Mercy, on his left, and Truth stands directly facing him. When a man enters his presence for judgment,

---

[9] The Pseudepigrapha are a collection of Jewish writings that are extra-Biblical and apocalyptic in nature.

a staff as it were, extends toward him from the splendor of Mercy and takes a position in front of him. At once the man falls prostrate, and all the angels of destruction fear and shrink from him.

3 Enoch 31.2

At this point, Mordecai tells Esther some of the most profound words of scripture. Esther has remained silent about being Jewish, as she was instructed by Mordecai.[10] Neither the king nor Haman knows her nationality. Mordecai assures Esther that if she remains silent she will perish, but G-d will bring deliverance to the Jews one way or the other.

And they told Mordecai Esther's words: Then Mordecai commanded to answer Esther, Think not yourself that in the king's palace you shall escape, any more than all the Jews: For if you remain silent at this time, then shall relief and deliverance arise to the Jews from another place; but you and your father's house shall be destroyed; And who knows whether you have not come to the kingdom for such a time as this:

Esther 4.12-14

Esther was indeed placed in the royal house by G-d for such a time as this. Esther makes a request of Mordecai and the Jews of Shushan; that they fast and pray for three days with her before she approaches the king. Each year since that time Jews throughout the world have fasted in commemoration of this request. This is known as *Taanit Esther* or the Fast of Esther on the 13th of Adar; although, Esther fasted from the 14th till the 16th of Nisan, during the Passover season.

Go, gather together all the Jews who are present in Shushan, and fast for me, and neither eat nor drink

---

[10] Esther 2.10, 20

PRIDE AND EVIL

> three days, night or day; I also and my girls will fast likewise; and so will I go to the king, though it is against the law; and if I perish, I perish:
>
> Esther 4.16

G-d brings about His redemption of the Jewish people through His agents, Esther and Mordecai. These events begin to unfold as Esther approaches King Ahasuerus at his royal court on the 16th of Nisan. During this audience, she requests that the king and Haman attend a banquet at her house that same day.

> And it came to pass on the third day, that Esther put on her royal dress, and stood in the inner court of the king's palace, opposite the king's palace; and the king sat upon his royal throne in the royal palace, opposite the gate of the house: And it was so, when the king saw Esther the queen standing in the court, that she found favor in his sight; and the king held out to Esther the golden scepter that was in his hand; So Esther drew near, and touched the top of the scepter:
>
> Esther 5.1-2

This is another picture of how the grace of G-d is presented to the individual who comes asking for life. It is important to remember, although Esther was very frightened, she appeared before the king with proper decorum. Her obedience and courtly manner are examples to all believers on how to approach the throne of G-d.

> And Esther answered, If it seem good to the king, let the king and Haman come this day to the banquet that I have prepared for him:
>
> Esther 5.4

PROPHECIES IN THE BOOK OF ESTHER

This is exactly how G-d works to provide the means of a solution before a problem is actually manifested. So often, as in this case, people cannot see that G-d has everything under control. There is a tendency to focus on the problem rather than focusing on the deliverance of G-d. As far as the Jewish people are concerned, no power on earth or in heaven will ever be able to displace what G-d has promised.

If those ordinances depart from before me, says the L-rd, then the seed of Israel also shall cease from being a nation before me forever: Thus says the L-rd; If heaven above can be measured, and the foundations of the earth explored below, then I will also cast off all the seed of Israel for all that they have done, says the L-rd: Behold, the days come, says the L-rd, when the city shall be built to the L-rd from the Tower of Hananeel to the Corner's Gate:

Jeremiah 31.35-37

6. Dinner

> And it came to pass on the third day, that Esther put on her royal dress, and stood in the inner court of the king's palace, opposite the king's palace; and the king sat upon his royal throne in the royal palace, opposite the gate of the house:
>
> Esther 5.1

It is now the 16th of Nisan. The fasting and praying have been done. The queen undoubtedly takes great pains to beautify herself as she prepares to lay her life on the line in approaching the king. The walk to his court must have been incredibly long for the stakes were so high. Within her mind, Esther possibly had thoughts of how this same king had deposed Vashti for refusing to obey his command. To approach the king without being summoned could be interpreted as a queen declaring her independence and rebelling against her husband and king. However, Esther has no choice, for the salvation of her people lies with what occurs at this crucial moment.

> And it was so, when the king saw Esther the queen standing in the court, that she found favor in his sight; and the king held out to Esther the golden scepter that was in his hand; So Esther drew near, and touched the top of the scepter:
>
> Esther 5.2

Instead of observing a woman that is in rebellion, King Ahasuerus saw a true queen that had risked her life in approaching him. What a total opposite to Vashti who refused to appear at his bidding. The golden scepter (which represents grace, life, and the Messiah) are extended to her. From this point, Haman's hours are numbered even though he is totally unaware of it.

PROPHECIES IN THE BOOK OF ESTHER

> Then said the king to her, What do you wish, queen Esther? and what is your request? It shall be given to you even to the half of the kingdom: And Esther answered, If it seem good to the king, let the king and Haman come this day to the banquet that I have prepared for him: Then the king said, Make Haman hurry, that he may do as Esther has said; So the king and Haman came to the banquet that Esther had prepared:
>
> Esther 5.3-5

The king is so impressed he offers up to half his kingdom.[1] Esther's request, which appears to be for the sole purpose of honoring both the king and Haman, must have been incredibly flattering to Ahasuerus. The king was probably at the height of his love for Esther, a woman who would risk her life to honor him.

> And the king said to Esther at the banquet of wine, What is your petition? and it shall be granted you; and what is your request? even to the half of the kingdom it shall be granted: Then answered Esther, and said, My petition and my request is: If I have found favor in the sight of the king, and if it please the king to grant my petition, and to grant my request, let the king and Haman come to the banquet that I shall prepare for them, and I will do tomorrow as the king has said:
>
> Esther 5.6-8

Again, the date of this banquet is the 16th of Nisan. For the second time, Ahasuerus offers Esther up to half his kingdom, although her only request is that she entertains the two men at an additional banquet on the following day, the 17th of Nisan. She further states that at that banquet she will do as the king has said, state her petition. Esther was appealing to the king. Although he

---

[11] Romans 8.17; 2 Timothy 2.12

DINNER

undoubtedly had a harem filled with lovely women, Ahasuerus was excited about his prospects with Esther. Haman, on the other hand, was eager to broadcast his stature with everyone. He appeared to be truly blessed and appreciated by the court, yet all became nothing to him because of his contempt for Mordecai.

> Then went Haman out that day joyful and with a glad heart; but when Haman saw Mordecai in the king's gate, that he did not stand nor stir for him, he was full of indignation against Mordecai: And Haman refrained himself; and when he came home, he sent and called for his friends, and Zeresh his wife: And Haman told them of the glory of his riches, and the multitude of his children, and all the things by which the king had promoted him, and how he had advanced him above the princes and servants of the king: And Haman said, And Esther the queen did let no man come in with the king to the banquet that she had prepared but myself; and tomorrow I am also invited to her with the king: Yet all this avails me nothing, so long as I see Mordecai the Jew sitting at the king's gate:
>
> Esther 5.9-13

Haman's pride is evident as he journeys home, yet as he sees Mordecai, who refuses to bow before him, his joy is numbed. This is how the anti-Semitic spirit, as well as pride, works. In like manner, the False Messiah of the future will be blinded by his anti-Semitic rage, and in the midst of all of his problems make war against the Children of Israel[2] which corporately as a nation become followers of Yeshua the Messiah.[3]

---

[2] Daniel 7.25; Revelation 13.7
[3] Ezekiel 39.22; Isaiah 10.12, 20-23; Romans 11.25; Revelation 12.13-17

PROPHECIES IN THE BOOK OF ESTHER

> And Zeresh his wife and all his friends said to him, Let a gallows be made fifty cubits high, and tomorrow speak to the king that Mordecai may be hanged on it; then go in cheerfully with the king to the banquet; And the thing pleased Haman; and he had the gallows made:
>
> Esther 5.14

At last Haman had a solution. As he could not wait eleven months for Mordecai and the Jews to be exterminated, he delighted that within twenty-four hours he would be rid of Mordecai once and for all. Perhaps his plan kept him awake in anticipation. However, the king could not sleep for other reasons. G-d kept the king from sleep for a divine purpose.

> On that night the king could not sleep, and he commanded to bring the Book of Records of the Chronicles; and they were read before the king: And it was found written, that Mordecai had told of Bigthana and Teresh, two of the king's eunuchs, the keepers of the door, who sought to lay hand on the king Ahasuerus: And the king said, What honor and dignity has been done to Mordecai for this? Then said the king's servants who ministered to him, Nothing was done for him:
>
> Esther 6.1-3

All things now come to a head and Haman, who sought this day to destroy Mordecai, is caught in a web from which he cannot escape; so too will be the fate of the False Messiah. The scripture, as mentioned before, speaks of a *Sefer Zikaron,* Book of Remembrance[4] where G-d records all that we have done in righteousness. This mirrors the chronicles in which is recorded the deed of Mordecai saving Ahasuerus from assassination. Only Ahasuerus had forgotten to reward Mordecai. It was not in the plan of G-d for Mordecai to be

---

[4] Malachi 3.16

DINNER

rewarded until this time. Often it is not evident how G-d operates in believers' lives, yet there is the assurance that all works to the good of the believer, and the Kingdom of G-d.[5]

> And the king said, Who is in the court? Now Haman had come into the outward court of the king's palace, to speak to the king to hang Mordecai on the gallows that he had prepared for him: And the king's servants said to him, Behold, Haman stands in the court; And the king said, Let him come in: So Haman came in; And the king said to him, What shall be done to the man whom the king delights to honor? Now Haman thought in his heart, To whom would the king delight to do honor more than to myself:
>
> Esther 6.4-6

How strange that Haman would arrive at the king's court at a time that the king should be already asleep. Even as the king was unable to sleep by the Spirit of G-d, so Haman is drawn to the palace by his impatience. Haman had already prepared the gallows to hang Mordecai. As Haman arrives, the king realizes that he has been grossly negligent concerning Mordecai. As the king questions Haman as to how to honor a deserving man in the court, Haman, in his pride, is convinced the reward is for him.

> And Haman answered the king, For the man whom the king delights to honor: Let the royal clothing be brought which the king wears, and the horse that the king rides upon, and the crown royal which is set upon his head: And let this clothing and horse be delivered to the hand of one of the king's most noble princes, that they may array the man with it whom the king delights to honor, and bring him on horseback through the street of the city, and proclaim before him, Thus shall it be done to the man whom

---

[5] Romans 8.28

PROPHECIES IN THE BOOK OF ESTHER

> the king delights to honor: Then the king said to Haman, Hurry, and take the clothing and the horse, as you have said, and do so to Mordecai the Jew, who sits at the king's gate; let nothing fail of all that you have spoken:
>
> Esther 6.7-10

Haman names the reward that he would most like to receive. In doing this, he names his own poison. Surely, Haman first glimpsed the beginning of his downfall. Haman's bitter disappointment must have weighed as heavily as a millstone tied around his neck as he heard the honor bestowed upon Mordecai.

> Then took Haman the clothing and the horse, and arrayed Mordecai, and brought him on horseback through the street of the city, and proclaimed before him, Thus shall it be done to the man whom the king delights to honor: And Mordecai came again to the king's gate; But Haman hurried to his house mourning, and having his head covered:
>
> Esther 6.11-12

The honor bestowed upon Mordecai is a reflection of the honor and coronation of the Messiah. Likewise, Haman's humiliation and servitude to Mordecai is a picture of the future dishonor of Satan and his False Messiah.

> And Haman told Zeresh his wife and all his friends everything that had befallen him; Then said his wise men and Zeresh his wife to him, If Mordecai, before whom you have begun to fall, is of the seed of the Jews you shall not prevail against him, but shall surely fall before him:
>
> Esther 6.13

DINNER

As Haman told his wife Zeresh and his friends who were present all that has transpired, his wife prophesied words that are reminiscent of G-d's words to Belshazzar, the Babylonian ruler.

> And this is the writing that was written, MENE, MENE, TEKEL, and PARSIN: This is the meaning of the matter; MENE; G-d has numbered your kingdom, and brought it to an end: TEKEL; You are weighed in the balances, and are found wanting: PERES; Your kingdom is divided, and given to the Medes and Persians:
>
> Daniel 5.25-28

The handwriting was on the wall. Just as the Babylonian Empire was overthrown by the Medes and Persians, Haman's downfall was imminent.

> And while they were still talking with him, came the king's eunuchs, and hurried to bring Haman to the banquet that Esther had prepared:
>
> Esther 6.14

It is remarkable how fast all the pieces of the puzzle in Haman's destruction came together. Haman must have been in a state of confusion and panic. So it will be for all those who follow Satan as Yeshua comes in power and glory.

PROPHECIES IN THE BOOK OF ESTHER

7. Just Desserts

> So the king and Haman came to feast with Esther the queen:
>
> Esther 7.1

As the king and Haman prepare to dine with the queen, Haman has no clue to the delicate position into which he has ignorantly placed himself. To dine privately in the presence of a king and queen, this was more than most men of Haman's stature could ever hope to achieve. At this time, we enter into an ordained time set by G-d. From this point forward, Haman's "favor" is completely reversed.

> And the king said again to Esther on the second day at the banquet of wine, What is your petition, queen Esther? and it shall be granted you; and what is your request? and it shall be fulfilled, even to the half of the kingdom: Then Esther the queen answered and said, If I have found favor in your sight, O king, and if it please the king, let my life be given me at my petition, and my people at my request:
>
> Esther 7.2-3

For the third time, Ahasuerus offers to give Esther whatever she would desire up to half the kingdom. She then brings her true petition before the king, a petition requesting that her life and the lives of her people be spared from the annihilation that he had decreed.

> For we are sold, I and my people, to be destroyed, to be slain, and to be annihilated; But if we had been

PROPHECIES IN THE BOOK OF ESTHER

> sold as male and female slaves, I would have kept my silence, since the affliction would not have equaled the kings' damage:
>
> Esther 7.4

Esther's words concerning the Jewish people "to be destroyed, to be slain, and to perish" have been echoed through the centuries by numbers of different peoples, each caught in the Satanic trap of anti-Semitism. These words have never diminished in intensity, nor have they ever proved to be expressions without intent by those who have voiced them. Similarly, the ancient Psalmist quoted numbers of surrounding nations who were Israel's enemies:

> A Song Psalm of Asaph:
>
> Do not keep silent, O G-d; do not hold your peace and be still, O G-d: For, behold, your enemies make a tumult; and those who hate you have lifted up the head: They have taken crafty counsel against your people, and consulted against your hidden ones: They have said, Come, and let us cut them off from being a nation; that the name of Israel may no longer be remembered: For they conspire together with one accord; they make an alliance against you: The tents of Edom, and the Ishmaelites; of Moab, and the Hagarites: Gebal, and Ammon, and Amalek; the Philistines with the inhabitants of Tyre: Assyria also has joined them; they are the strong arm of the children of Lot; Selah:
>
> Psalms 83.1-9 (83.1-8)

The covenant of the Palestinian Liberation Organization has expressions that parallel those above both from the book of Esther as well as the Psalm. In this covenant, the Palestinians are devoted to

JUST DESSERTS

the destruction of Israel and the Jewish people.[1] Although the PLO no longer exists in name, the Palestinian Authority has kept the covenant intact and refused to change the context, even while peace negotiations with Israel continue to take place.

> And the king Ahasuerus answered and said to Esther the queen, Who is he, and where is he, that does presume in his heart to do so: And Esther said, The adversary and enemy is this wicked Haman;
>
> Esther 7.5–6a

Immediately the situation is reversed as the king cries "Who is he, and where is he!" After all, who would dare to threaten his own queen and her family? King Ahasuerus, who is believed to have been the Persian King Xerxes the Great, was famous for his incredible temper.[2] The king's outrage must have echoed within the palace walls as he heard her plea.

It is interesting to imagine the racing thoughts of Haman at this time, for until she petitions the king for her life, he had not known that Esther too was the target of his evil plot. It may have occurred to him as to who would be so foolish to attack the highly favored queen. Upon hearing her words, his bowels surely turned to water. Where now were his well-laid plans for advancing in the kingdom and his revenge upon Mordecai? It is probable Haman still did not know that Mordecai was related to the Queen.

> Then Haman was afraid before the king and the queen: And the king arising from the banquet of wine in his wrath went to the palace garden; and Haman stood up to beg Esther the queen for his life; for he saw that there was evil determined against him by

---

[1] The National Covenant of the Palestinian Liberation Organization, Articles 19 and 21.
[2] Xerxes upon being defeated by Greek warships in the battle of Salamis decreed that the Mediterranean Sea be flogged.

> the king: Then the king returned from the palace garden to the place of the wine drinking; and Haman was falling upon the couch where Esther was; Then said the king, Will he also force the queen with me present in the house?
>
> Esther 7.6b–8c

Haman's nightmare continued to increase from this point, as the king was in such a rage that he could not stay in the room. Haman knew that he was in dire straits. While Esther was on a couch,[3] Haman, in mortal fear, fell across the couch sniveling for his life as the king re-entered the room. Things could not have been worse for Haman, as no man would even dare to carelessly touch the queen. The penalty would be certain death. The grotesque vision the king witnessed gave the impression of Haman sexually attacking the queen within the king's own domain. This is possibly the most graphic picture in scripture that shows the fear that Satan and his False Messiah will experience as they come against the wrath of the Almighty G-d.

It is difficult to envision this scene without recalling the words of the psalmist;

> Give them according to their deeds, and according to the wickedness of their endeavors: give them after the work of their hands; render to them their desert.
>
> Psalm 28.4

Now in addition to premeditated murder, what appeared to be the attempted rape of his queen, the king's chosen bride, is added to Haman's list of offenses.

---

[3] The "bed" spoken of here is really a couch which was the Persian custom for feasting; Esther 1.6; A. H. Layard, the pioneer archeologist in Assyrian, Babylonian and Persian studies states "chairs and couches adorned with feet of silver and other metals were looked upon as a great object of luxury in Persia." (Layard, 1849, pp. 300, Vol 2).

JUST DESSERTS

> As the word went out of the king's mouth, they covered Haman's face: And Harbonah, one of the eunuchs, said before the king, Behold also, the gallows fifty cubits high, which Haman had made for Mordecai, who had spoken good for the king, stands in the house of Haman; Then the king said, Hang him on it:
>
> Esther 7.8d – 9

When Harbonah, one of the king's chamberlains, had gone to escort Haman to the banquet earlier,[4] he had seen the gallows on Haman's property and apparently knew that they were intended for Mordecai. This same servant appears to have been in the presence of the king when the chronicles were read detailing Mordecai's deed of saving Ahasuerus' life and the king's desire to honor him.[5] In conjunction with the king's words to hang Haman on the gallows built for Mordecai is a passage from the Torah.

> And if a man has committed a sin deserving death, and he is to be put to death, and you hang him on a tree: His body shall not remain all night upon the tree, but you shall bury him that day; for he who is hanged is accursed by G-d; that your land, which the L-rd your G-d gives you for an inheritance, be not defiled:
>
> Deuteronomy 21.22-23

Haman's face was quickly covered by the king's men as was the custom of the Persians. Someone who was to be executed or who displeased the king would have their face covered by a veil or napkin, marking the beginning of carrying out the sentence of death into execution.[6] Haman was repaid according to the

---

[4] Esther 6.14
[5] Esther 6.4-5
[6] (Robert Jamieson, 1999)

PROPHECIES IN THE BOOK OF ESTHER

wickedness of his endeavors and received his just desserts.[7] The destruction he planned for others, he reaped for himself.

> So they hanged Haman on the gallows that he had prepared for Mordecai; Then was the king's wrath pacified:
>
> Esther 7.10

As Haman hung on the gallows, the king's wrath abated. Even so, as Satan and the False Messiah are judged G-d's wrath will be pacified.

---

[7] Psalms 7.15-16

8. The 17th Day of Nisan

Haman finally received his death sentence and was hung. Note that Haman died on the 17th of Nisan. This specific date is profoundly used throughout scripture as an anniversary of a multitude of events. How remarkable that this day of defeat for Satan and those who are like-minded with Haman is a day of victory for the people of G-d.

The month's name, Nisan, is used interchangeably throughout scripture with the name, Aviv. Both Nisan and Aviv are synonymous and are in fact the same month. Prior to Exodus 12, Nisan (Aviv) was the seventh month of the calendar; however, following the institution of the Passover sacrifice in Egypt, the calendar was changed to reflect the new year beginning in the spring with Nisan/Aviv.[1] Events in scripture that occurred in the month of Nisan/Aviv prior to the slaying of the Passover lamb in Exodus 12 would have been reckoned to have occurred in the seventh month. From Exodus 12 and onward, Nisan/Aviv is considered as the first month of the year. This insight helps us to understand the importance of being familiar with the months of the Jewish calendar. For example, by context, we can identify whether the scriptures are speaking of the first or seventh month.

The events in the story of Esther take place over these very important days. Included below are a few examples of other profound events that took place on the 17th of Aviv. As always, prophecy confirms itself with biblical documentation. What has happened before happened more than once and will ultimately occur again.

---

[1] Exodus 12.2; Exodus 13.4; Deuteronomy 16.1

PROPHECIES IN THE BOOK OF ESTHER

Noah's Ark

> And the ark rested in the seventh month, on the seventeenth day of the month, upon the mountains of Ararat:
>
> Genesis 8.4

It is difficult to imagine how the eight people in the ark felt when the ark touched the ground for the first time. They knew that everyone outside the ark had perished. At times they may have thought that they would surely perish too. All that sustained them was confidence in G-d according to His promises that they would live, but the reality of the accomplishment of these promises became manifest on the 17th of Nisan.

The Parting of the Red Sea

> And the people of Israel went into the midst of the sea upon the dry ground; and the waters were a wall to them on their right hand, and on their left: And the Egyptians pursued, and went in after them to the midst of the sea, all Pharaoh's horses, his chariots, and his horsemen: And it came to pass, that in the morning watch the L-rd looked to the army of the Egyptians through the pillar of fire and of the cloud, and brought confusion to the army of the Egyptians: And took off their chariot wheels, that they drove heavily; so that the Egyptians said, Let us flee from the face of Israel; for the L-rd fights for them against the Egyptians: And the L-rd said to Moses, Stretch out your hand over the sea, that the waters may come again upon the Egyptians, upon their chariots, and upon their horsemen: And Moses stretched forth his hand over the sea, and the sea returned to his strength when the morning appeared; and the Egyptians fled towards it; and the L-rd overthrew the

THE 17TH DAY OF NISAN

> Egyptians in the midst of the sea: And the waters returned, and covered the chariots, and the horsemen, and all the army of Pharaoh that came into the sea after them; there remained not so much as one of them: But the people of Israel walked upon dry land in the midst of the sea; and the waters were a wall to them on their right hand, and on their left: Thus the L-rd saved Israel that from the hand of the Egyptians; and Israel saw the Egyptians dead upon the sea shore:
>
> Exodus 14.22-30

One of the greatest events in history took place in the book of Exodus. The Children of Israel left Egypt on the night of the 15th of Nisan, traveled for three days to the sea, and arrived to cross the sea on the 17th of Nisan. In the above scripture, Moses is seen as a picture of the Messiah and Pharaoh is likewise a picture of Satan and the False Messiah. Unlike many movies that attempt to bring these events to life, scripture records that Pharaoh went into the sea with his troops and drowned.[2] Just as Pharaoh, a type of the False Messiah, perished, the Children of Israel came up alive out of the depths of the sea. What a parallel to Haman's death on the 17th of Nisan. Not only is this the day that Haman dies, but it is the date that the king sends out a new edict to the entire Persian world proclaiming the right of the Jews to defend themselves. It is now evident they will be delivered at a future date.

> And made Israel pass through the midst of it; for his loving kindness endures for ever: And overthrew Pharaoh and his army in the Red Sea; for his loving kindness endures for ever:
>
> Psalms 136.14-15

---

[2] Psalm 136.15

PROPHECIES IN THE BOOK OF ESTHER

His mercy does endure forever, even when the object of His great love, Israel, rebels, and sins. This was the case in Israel before Hezekiah became king.

King Hezekiah

> He, in the first year of his reign, in the first month, opened the doors of the house of the L-rd, and repaired them:
>
> 2 Chronicles 29.3

King Hezekiah, who the rabbis taught was a type of the Messiah, began his reign by rededicating the Holy Temple. He also called the people to walk in righteousness before G-d.

> Now it is in my heart to make a covenant with the L-rd G-d of Israel, that his fierce wrath may turn away from us: My sons, do not be now negligent; for the L-rd has chosen you to stand before him, to serve him, and that you should minister to him, and burn incense:
>
> 2 Chronicles 29.10-11

Hezekiah strengthened the priesthood in their holy commission to lead the people in their worship of G-d. In addition, he divided the priesthood into their orders, just as King David had done. In this way, the priesthood and the maintenance of the Temple were set in order.

> And they gathered their brothers, and sanctified themselves, and came, according to the commandment of the king, by the words of the L-rd, to cleanse the house of the L-rd: And the priests went into the inner part of the house of the L-rd, to cleanse it, and they brought out all the uncleanness that they found in the temple of the L-rd into the court of the house of the L-rd; And the Levites took it, to

THE 17TH DAY OF NISAN

> carry it out to the brook Kidron: And they began on the first day of the first month to sanctify, and on the eighth day of the month they came to the vestibule of the L-rd; so they sanctified the house of the L-rd in eight days; and in the sixteenth day of the first month they finished: And they went inside to Hezekiah the king, and said, We have cleansed all the house of the L-rd, and the altar of the burnt offering, with all its utensils, and the table of the bread of display, with all its utensils: And all the utensils, which king Ahaz in his reign cast away in his transgression, have we prepared and sanctified, and, behold, they are before the altar of the L-rd:
>
> 2 Chronicles 29.15-19

Hezekiah sent the priests to cleanse the Temple, which had been desecrated by his father, Ahaz. They completed their work on the 16th of Nisan and reported back to Hezekiah.

> And Hezekiah the king rose early, and gathered the rulers of the city, and went up to the house of the L-rd:
>
> 2 Chronicles 29.20

On the 17th of Nisan Hezekiah rose early in the morning even as the Children of Israel came up out of the sea early in the morning. It is important to remember that the scriptures were inspired by G-d in order to communicate and teach. His Word also shows that G-d keeps His divine appointments.

> And the service of the house of the L-rd was restored: And Hezekiah rejoiced, and all the people, because of what G-d had done for the people; for the thing was done suddenly:
>
> 2 Chronicles 29.35b-36

On this same day, King Hezekiah rose early in the morning following the cleansing of the Temple desecrated by his father, King

PROPHECIES IN THE BOOK OF ESTHER

Ahaz. The king took with him all the nobles of the land and a great celebration of the glory of G-d took place. His father had been a picture of Satan and the Temple in ruins had shown the world in its fallen state. Throughout this chapter in Second Chronicles, one of the greatest celebrations before G-d is described. This celebration and all other events on this day are to teach on the celebration that took place in heaven as restoration was brought back to the universe. This restoration also took place on the 17th of Nisan, and it became the greatest day of defeat for Satan, the day Yeshua rose from the dead.

The Resurrection of Yeshua

It becomes obvious that as Yeshua faced His death on the 14th of Nisan, the day of Passover, remains in the grave for three days and three nights,[3] that his resurrection took place on the 17th of Nisan. It is written that the parting of the Red Sea took place in the morning[4] even as Hezekiah rose early in the morning. These events provide a clue to the highly controversial time of the resurrection of Yeshua.

Even as Hezekiah took many of the nobles up with him to the Temple,[5] so did Yeshua raise many of the righteous ones at His own resurrection, early in the morning.[6] Yeshua rose from the grave just before daybreak.

> The first day of the week cometh Mary Magdalene early, when it was yet dark, unto the sepulchre, and seeth the stone taken away from the sepulchre.
>
> John 20.1

Haman's fate on the 17th of Nisan was no accident or coincidence. His downfall, defeat, and death on this date show a perfect picture of G-d's judgment and mercy. The ensuing events

---

[3] Matthew 12.39-40
[4] Exodus 14.24
[5] 2 Chronicles 29.20
[6] Matthew 27.51-53

THE 17TH DAY OF NISAN

following his execution are characteristic of G-d's redemption. Mordecai's elevation on this same day reveals the redemptive and Messianic message of this work of G-d.

Even as Haman's end unfolds in the story of Esther, there is more to come, an epilogue to his climatic ruin. The story is not complete until the enemy is completely deposed and restoration is provided.

PROPHECIES IN THE BOOK OF ESTHER

9. Justice

> On that day the king Ahasuerus gave the house of Haman the Jews' enemy to Esther the queen; And Mordecai came before the king; for Esther had told what he was to her: And the king took off his ring, which he had taken from Haman, and gave it to Mordecai; And Esther set Mordecai over the house of Haman:
>
> Esther 8.1-2

Throughout the centuries the teachers of Israel have interpreted the expression "On that day" as being an eschatological reference to the Messianic Kingdom or the Millennium. King Ahasuerus gives all that was Haman's to Esther, who turned it over to Mordecai; even as all that was Satan's and his False Messiah's will be given to Yeshua.

The following passage from Ezekiel speaks of the False Messiah, the profane wicked prince of Israel, being stripped of his possessions. All authority and titles will be bestowed on the Messiah.

> And you, profane wicked prince of Israel, whose day has come, when iniquity shall have an end: Thus says the L-rd G-d; Remove the turban, and take off the crown; things shall not be the same; exalt him who is low, and abase him who is high: A ruin, a ruin, a ruin will I make it; and it shall be no more, until he comes whose right it is; and I will give it to him:
>
> Ezekiel 21.30-32 (21.25-27)

Another comment on Esther 8.1-2 relates to the phrase that "Mordecai came before the king." The prophet Daniel spoke of the day of the coronation of the Son of Man, the Messiah.

PROPHECIES IN THE BOOK OF ESTHER

> I saw in the night visions, and, behold, one like a son of man came with the clouds of heaven, and came to the ancient of days, and they brought him near before him: And there he was given dominion, and glory, and a kingdom, that all people, nations, and languages, should serve him; his dominion is an everlasting dominion, which shall not pass away, and his kingdom one that shall not be destroyed:
>
> Daniel 7.13-14

The 17th of Nisan is a great day for the Jews. Haman, their enemy, has been executed and Mordecai has been elevated in the kingdom. However, Haman's decree for the destruction of the Jews is still a reality to be dealt with. Esther approached the king about this matter also.

> And Esther spoke once more before the king, and fell down at his feet, and pleaded with tears to avert the evil design of Haman the Agagite, and his plot that he had devised against the Jews: Then the king held out the golden scepter toward Esther; So Esther arose, and stood before the king: And said, If it please the king, and if I have found favor in his sight, and the thing seem right before the king, and if I am pleasing in his eyes, let it be decreed to revoke the letters devised by Haman the son of Hammedatha the Agagite, which he wrote to destroy the Jews who are in all the king's provinces: For how can I endure to see the evil that shall come to my people? or how can I endure to see the destruction of my kindred:
>
> Esther 8.3-6

As Esther came before the King, she approached him in humility and tears on behalf of her people. Ahasuerus once again extended the golden scepter. When Esther rose before the scepter, she brought the petition to revoke the decree of Haman. In Esther's example of approaching Ahasuerus in such humility and respect for the king, G-d has given a model in how to approach His Throne.

JUSTICE

Often people feel that to pray to the Almighty is best expressed in making demands of Him. The following example of Esther's approach to the throne should be noted:

1. She fell at his feet and sought him with tears,

2. She rose only after the scepter was presented,

3. She asked, "If it pleases the king ..."

4. She sought his favor with reverence,

5. She asked that her petition be in his will, and

6. She prepared herself to look pleasing.

Even today it would be unseemly to make demands, turn one's back on, or approach a monarch discourteously. If such great pains were taken in the days of the ancient monarchs, how much more should be observed when one approaches the throne of G-d?

> Then the king Ahasuerus said to Esther the queen and to Mordecai the Jew, Behold, I have given Esther the house of Haman, and him they have hanged upon the gallows, because he would lay his hand upon the Jews: And you write about the Jews, as you please, in the king's name, and seal it with the king's ring; for the decrees which are decreed in the king's name, and sealed with the king's ring, no man can revoke:
>
> Esther 8.7-8

PROPHECIES IN THE BOOK OF ESTHER

According to the laws of the Medes and the Persians, once a decree had been sealed with the signet ring of the king, it was impossible to reverse.[1]

Therefore; Ahasuerus instructs Esther and Mordecai to write a decree to counter Haman's. This is reminiscent of the principle that G-d's Name or His word not be used in vain or made null and void. An example of this is found in the book of Genesis as Isaac cannot withdraw his blessing given to Jacob, even though he had meant to bestow the blessing upon Esau.[2] Likewise, a king's seal could not be considered void. Once Haman had written the law in the name of the king that the Jews were to be annihilated, the decree could not be revoked; they would be attacked on the 13th of Adar. In order to save the Jews, a new decree had to be written as a counter for the first.

> Then were the king's scribes called at that time in the third month, that is, the month Sivan, on its twenty third day; And it was written according to all that Mordecai commanded to the Jews, and to the satraps, and the governors and the princes of the provinces which are from Hodu to Kush, one hundred twenty and seven provinces, to every province according to its writing, and to every people in their own language, and to the Jews according to their writing, and according to their language:

> Esther 8.9

Why did Mordecai and Esther wait until 23 Sivan, more than two months, to write their decree and send it out? The rabbis taught that it was to allow the original couriers of Haman to return from their trips of the 13th of Nisan. By using the same couriers, this would thereby reinforce the validity of the decree of Mordecai and communicate effectively throughout the extensive empire the change

---

[1] Daniel 6.6-8,15
[2] Genesis 27.34-40

JUSTICE

of events in Shushan.

> And he wrote in king Ahasuerus' name, and sealed it with the king's ring, and sent letters by couriers on horseback, riding on the swift horses used in the royal service, bred from the royal mares: By these the king authorized the Jews who were in every city to gather themselves together, and to stand for their life, to destroy, to slay, and to annihilate, any armed force of any people or province that might attack them, infants and women, and to plunder their goods: On one day in all the provinces of king Ahasuerus, on the thirteenth day of the twelfth month, which is the month Adar:
>
> Esther 8.10-12

With the decree of Mordecai, the Jews were able to defend themselves. In addition, it was now known that Mordecai was both favored and next to the king and that the enemy of the Jews was dead. Those who sought the favor of the king would stand with the Jews against those who were of the spirit of Haman.

> But they shall sit in judgment, and his dominion shall be taken away, to be consumed and to be destroyed to the end: And the kingdom and the dominion, and the greatness of the kingdoms under the whole heaven, shall be given to the people of the holy ones of the most High, whose kingdom shall be an everlasting kingdom, and all dominions shall serve and obey him:
>
> Daniel 7.26-27

Earlier in the book of Daniel, scripture says "the court was seated..." which is the heavenly court where the Ancient of Days, sits. There will be a decree that will reach the entire earth, sent by

PROPHECIES IN THE BOOK OF ESTHER

heavenly couriers, angels, announcing that the Kingdom of G-d and the Messiah have arrived.[3]

> The copy of the written command to be issued as a decree in every province, and to be proclaimed to all peoples, and that the Jews should be ready against that day to avenge themselves on their enemies: So the couriers who rode on horseback, riding on the swift horses used in the royal service, hurried and pressed on by the king's command; And the decree was given at Shushan the capital:
>
> Esther 8.13.14

After issuing the second decree proclaiming the salvation of the Jews, Mordecai departed from the presence of the king in his royal attire. In a like manner, Yeshua will be seen as the King of Israel traveling in the greatness of His strength.

> And Mordecai went out from the presence of the king in royal clothes of blue and white, and with a great crown of gold, and with a garment of fine linen and purple; and the city of Shushan rejoiced and was glad: The Jews had light, and gladness, and joy, and honor:
>
> Esther 8.15-16

Throughout the empire, the Jews rejoiced because their ruin had become their victory and glory. The gentiles were in awe at this turn of events, so much so that many became Jews.

---

[3] Revelation 19.6-21

JUSTICE

Duplicitous Gog – Then & Now

(Here we Gog again like a Gog in a Wheel)

A parallel turn-of-events is the prophesied invasion of Israel by the armies of Gog. While topics such as Armageddon and the Anti-Christ are of high interest to Christian audiences and are the subject of countless articles, books, movies and sermons, it is the "War of Gog and Magog" which piques Jewish attention.

Gog and Magog are seen on two different levels in the Jewish writings. The first level is where the term "Gog and Magog" is directed towards any enemy of the Jewish people (similar to how the term "Amalek" is applied). This may be used toward an individual such as a president or ruler of a country, an organization, or a movement such as radical Islam. The second level of interpretation is a literal understanding of Ezekiel 38 and 39 when a great alliance from the north invades and brings devastation to Israel in the *Acharit Yamim* (Latter Days).

> Now the word of the L-RD came to me, saying, "Son of man, set your face against Gog, of the land of Magog, the prince of Rosh, Meshech, and Tubal, and prophesy against him, "and say, `Thus says the L-rd G-D: "Behold, I *am* against you, O Gog, the prince of Rosh, Meshech, and Tubal. "I will turn you around, put hooks into your jaws, and lead you out, with all your army, horses, and horsemen, all splendidly clothed, a great company *with* bucklers and shields, all of them handling swords. "Persia, Ethiopia, and Libya are with them, all of them *with* shield and helmet; "Gomer and all its troops; the house of Togarmah *from* the far north and all its troops-- many people *are* with you.
>
> Ezekiel 38.1-6 NKJ

The impact and significance of this war was developed through

PROPHECIES IN THE BOOK OF ESTHER

numerous avenues of the ancient Jewish writings such as the Talmud,[4] Midrash,[5] the Pseudepigrapha and Apocrypha,[6] and Jewish liturgy. The Pseudepigrapha and Apocrypha are numerous Jewish writings written between 200 BCE and 100 CE that were not included within the canon of the Tanach.[7] These books are very valuable as they reveal much about the Jewish people during this period and how they interpreted Biblical topics and episodes; they are historical, insightful and even prophetic in their content. In these writings the warfare against Gog and Magog formed the indispensable prelude to the Messianic era in every apocalyptic vision

By the First Century CE, the time of Yeshua, a set pattern of reading of the scriptures had been in use for some time. There was and continues to be a reading from the Torah known as a *Parshah* going progressively through the Torah week by week with the readings beginning the day following Sukkot (Tabernacles) known as *Shemini Atzeret/Simchat Torah* and concluding during this same festival.

There continues to be special readings from the Torah for the festivals. These special readings are read on the High Sabbaths that begin and end the Festivals of *Hag haMatzah* (Unleavened Bread), *Shavuot* (Weeks), *Rosh haShanah*, *Yom Kippur* (Day of Atonement) *Sukkot* and *Shemini Atzeret* (Eighth Day).[8] Three of the above Festivals, *Hag haMatzah*, *Shavuot* and *Sukkot* last for a week. As

---

[4] Avodah Zarah 3a-3b, Sanhedrin 17a-17b, Sanhedrin 47a-47b
[5] Midrash Tehillim Psalm 2
[6] Sibylline Oracles 3.319, 512, 632; 5.101, I Enoch 56.5, 2 Esdras 13.5, Syriac Apocalypse of Baruch 70.7-10
[7] The Jewish Scriptures
[8] *Shemini Atzeret* is a High Sabbath (Tishri 22) attached to Sukkot but distinct from it, for this reason it is known as the Eighth Day (1Kings 8.65-66). In Israel it also corresponds to Simchat Torah (the Rejoicing in the Torah) when the annual readings of the Torah start over for the year. In the Diaspora, Simchat Torah is celebrated on the next day (Tishri 23), but in Israel it coincides with Shemini Atzeret.

JUSTICE

mentioned before, the day the festival begins is called a "High Sabbath" or "*Shabbaton*" regardless of the day of the week of its occurrence. The days between the starting and concluding points (when it is not a High Sabbath) are known as *Chol haMoed* or the "Intermediate Days of the Festival". During these days people can go to their jobs, spend money and do all of the activities they normally do as it is not a Shabbat. During these Intermediate Days there is a weekly Shabbat. This Shabbat during Sukkot was known as *Shabbat Chol haMoed Sukkot*.

With each weekly and Festival Torah reading there is an accompanying reading from the Prophets called the *Haftarah*. Today, as during the time of Yeshua, the *Haftarah* for *Shabbat Chol haMoed Sukkot* is Ezekiel 38.18-39.16.

> R. Huna said in the name of R. Shesheth: **On the Sabbath which falls in the intermediate days of the festival, whether Passover or Tabernacles**, the passage we read from the Torah is 'See, Thou [sayest unto me]' and for haftarah on Passover the passage of the 'dry bones', **and on Tabernacles, 'In that day when Gog shall come'**.
> Megillah 31.a[9]

In the account from Ezekiel a great northern alliance headed by Gog of the land of Magog invades Israel with an overwhelming army, sweeps through the land destroying the Jewish people and their land.

> "You will ascend, coming like a storm, covering the land like a cloud, you and all your troops and many peoples with you." `Thus says the L-rd G-D: "On that day it shall come to pass *that* thoughts will arise in your mind, and you will make an evil plan: "You will say, `I will go up against a land of unwalled villages; I

---

[9] (David Kanhowitz, 2001) Emphasis is mine.

PROPHECIES IN THE BOOK OF ESTHER

> will go to a peaceful people, who dwell safely, all of them dwelling without walls, and having neither bars nor gates'-- "to take plunder and to take booty, to stretch out your hand against the waste places *that are again* inhabited, and against a people gathered from the nations, who have acquired livestock and goods, who dwell in the midst of the land. "Sheba, Dedan, the merchants of Tarshish, and all their young lions will say to you, `Have you come to take plunder? Have you gathered your army to take booty, to carry away silver and gold, to take away livestock and goods, to take great plunder?'" "Therefore, son of man, prophesy and say to Gog, `Thus says the L-rd G-D: "On that day when My people Israel dwell safely, will you not know *it*?" Then you will come from your place out of the far north, you and many peoples with you, all of them riding on horses, a great company and a mighty army. "You will come up against My people Israel like a cloud, to cover the land. It will be in the latter days that I will bring you against My land, so that the nations may know Me, when I am hallowed in you, O Gog, before their eyes."
>
> Ezekiel 38.9-16 NKJ

Josephus, the Jewish historian of the First Century CE identified the "land of Magog" with the Scythians, a nomadic horde of tribes that lived east of the Black Sea in present day Russia.

> For Gomer founded those whom the Greeks now call Galatians, [Galls,] but were then called Gomerites. Magog founded those who from him were named Magogites, but who are by the Greeks called Scythians.
>
> Antiquities of the Jews 1.123

When all seems to be lost and Israel seems defeated, the Jews will cry out to Hashem and He delivers them with quick justice in

JUSTICE

such a way that everyone will deem it a supernatural occurrence.

> "And it will come to pass at the same time, when Gog comes against the land of Israel," says the L-rd G-D, "*that* My fury will show in My face. "For in My jealousy *and* in the fire of My wrath I have spoken: `Surely in that day there shall be a great earthquake in the land of Israel, `so that the fish of the sea, the birds of the heavens, the beasts of the field, all creeping things that creep on the earth, and all men who *are* on the face of the earth shall shake at My presence. The mountains shall be thrown down, the steep places shall fall, and every wall shall fall to the ground.' "I will call for a sword against Gog throughout all My mountains," says the L-rd G-D. "Every man's sword will be against his brother." And I will bring him to judgment with pestilence and bloodshed; I will rain down on him, on his troops, and on the many peoples who *are* with him, flooding rain, great hailstones, fire, and brimstone. "Thus I will magnify Myself and sanctify Myself, and I will be known in the eyes of many nations. Then they shall know that I *am* the L-RD.'"
>
> Ezekiel 38.18-23 NKJ

The reason that this war yet to come has been at the forefront of Jewish expression is revealed in the following passage.

> "So the house of Israel shall know that I *am* the L-RD their G-d from that day forward.
>
> Ezekiel 39.22 NKJ

Now, knowing that this Haftarah was read during the intermediate days of Sukkot, the deliverance from Gog and Magog was certainly the topic of Yeshua's teaching that amazed the people who were at the Holy Temple. John notes it was during the

PROPHECIES IN THE BOOK OF ESTHER

Intermediate days of Sukkot when Ezekiel 38 and 39 would have been the teaching of the day.

> Now the Jews' Feast of Tabernacles (Sukkot) was at hand.
>
> John 7.2 NKJ

> Now about the middle of the feast Yeshua went up into the temple and taught. And the Jews marveled, saying, "How does this Man know letters, having never studied?" Yeshua answered them and said, "My doctrine is not Mine, but His who sent Me.
>
> John 7.14-16 NKJ

The similarities between the Jews' victory and deliverance over Haman, his sons and allies, and the triumph concerning Gog and Magog, are an example of the same story with a different cast. Once again, the pattern is repeated,

> And in every province, and in every city, wherever the king's command and his decree came, the Jews had joy and gladness, a feast and a good day; And many of the people of the land became Jews; for the fear of the Jews fell upon them:
>
> Esther 8.17

Now, all that remained was to wait for the appointed day of Adar the 13th, the day of redemption for the Jews when their enemies would be destroyed.

> Then I said, `Behold, I have come-- In the volume of the book it is written of Me-- To do Your will, O G-d.'"
>
> Hebrews 10.7 NKJ

10. Redemption

As stated earlier, the story of the redemption of the Jews in the Persian Empire did not stop with the death of Haman. In fact, the plight of the Jews would have to go the distance of time. It had been decreed that in the month of Adar, the Jews would be attacked. The eschatological implication of this month is significant. There are commonly two calendars referred to in scripture, the first beginning in Tishri, the anniversary of creation; and the second which begins with Nisan, the anniversary of Passover. Following Exodus 12, the latter calendar became the religious calendar, placing the first of the year in the spring. The former calendar which begins with *Rosh Hashanah* in the fall is the civil calendar and holds a great amount of spiritual significance. It is during this month of Tishri that the redemption of Israel is prophesied to occur.[1] The festivals of *Rosh Hashanah*, *Yom Kippur*, and *Sukkot*, all of which teach the timing and details of that redemption, take place in the month of Tishri. The time prior to this month is a time of repentance, a return to the ways of G-d and self-reflection.

The 50 days between Passover and Shavuot include the ritual of "counting the Omer."[2] The grain from the year's first wheat or barley harvest may not be eaten until the first fruits of that harvest are offered on Shavuot, which is why Shavuot is also called the *Festival of First Fruits*. The completion of those 50 days is eagerly awaited, especially by those running out of grain. Devout Jews introspectively examine their hearts during this same period for any trace of pride,

---

[1] Joel 2.23; (Eisemann, 1977, p. 580)
[2] Leviticus 23.15-16

PROPHECIES IN THE BOOK OF ESTHER

the sin of Haman. So the preparation for the time of repentance actually begins on the 16th of Nisan, the first day of the counting of the Omer.

The book of Esther refers to the first month of the year as Nisan as it was written after the event of the exodus. As Passover season occurs during this month, much preparation must be made. For example, all the leaven must be cleaned out of the home just prior to Passover as leaven is a picture of sin.[3] In addition, the entire home must be prepared, even before the casting out of all leaven, for the impending spring festivities. In a spiritual sense, before Passover, during the month of Adar is likewise a time of cleansing and removing sin from the lives of those who live according to the commandments of G-d.

If the calendar itself is a tool of G-d to teach the eschatology of what will happen, then the attack of the Jews at the end of the religious year during Adar, is actually a picture of what will happen at the end of days just before the Messiah returns bringing the prophesied peace.

> And in the twelfth month, that is, the month Adar, on the thirteenth day of the same, when the king's command and his decree drew near to be put in execution, in the day that the enemies of the Jews hoped to have power over them, though it was turned to the contrary, that the Jews had rule over those who hated them: The Jews gathered themselves together in their cities throughout all the provinces of the king Ahasuerus, to lay hand on such as sought their hurt; and no man could withstand them; for the fear of them fell upon all people: And all the rulers of the provinces, and the

---

[3] 1 Corinthians 5.6-8

REDEMPTION

satraps, and the governors, and the officials of the king, helped the Jews; because the fear of Mordecai had fallen upon them:

Esther 9.1-3

So it will be when Messiah returns and those who have faith in Him will be as warriors before the enemies of G-d. The following passages speak of that day when Messiah will return and the tables are turned against those of the False Messiah.

On that day, says the L-rd, I will strike every horse with panic, and its rider with madness; and I will open my eyes upon the house of Judah, and will strike every horse of the nations with blindness: And the governors of Judah shall say in their heart, The inhabitants of Jerusalem are my strength through the L-rd of hosts their G-d: On that day I will make the governors of Judah like a hearth of fire among trees, and like a torch of fire in a sheaf; and they shall devour all the peoples around, on the right hand and on the left; and Jerusalem shall be inhabited again in her own place, in Jerusalem: And the L-rd shall save the tents of Judah first, that the glory of the house of David and the glory of the inhabitants of Jerusalem do not magnify themselves against Judah: On that day shall the L-rd defend the inhabitants of Jerusalem; and he who is feeble among them shall be as David on that day; and the house of David shall be like a divine being, like the angel of the L-rd before them: And it shall come to pass on that day, that I will seek to destroy all the nations that come against Jerusalem:

Zechariah 12.4-9

PROPHECIES IN THE BOOK OF ESTHER

This passage reveals that each man, even the feeble, will become as David. Such was the case with Mordecai and the Jews in Persia. Just as the authority and power of Mordecai instituted fear among the people to do the Jews harm, so it will be in the future when Yeshua returns with all power and authority.[4]

> For Mordecai was great in the king's palace, and his fame went out throughout all the provinces; for this man Mordecai grew greater and greater:
>
> Esther 9.4

Following Yeshua's resurrection, His fame spread throughout the entire world, not only among the Jews, who during the First Century C. E. numbered in the tens of thousands.[5]

> Thus the Jews struck all their enemies with the stroke of the sword, and slaughter, and destruction, and did what they would to those who hated them:
>
> Esther 9.5

The details of the coming of the Messiah are given in many passages. One of the most profound is found in the Zechariah 14.

> Behold, the day of the L-rd comes, and the plunder taken from you shall be divided in your midst: For I will gather all nations against Jerusalem to battle; and the city shall be taken, and the houses rifled, and the women raped; and half of the city shall go into exile, and the remnant of the people shall not be cut off from the city: Then shall the L-rd go forth, and fight against those nations, as when he fought in the day of battle: And his feet shall stand on that day upon the Mount of Olives, which is before Jerusalem on the east, and the Mount of Olives shall be split in

---

[4] Isaiah 52.13-15
[5] Acts 21.20

REDEMPTION

> its midst toward the east and toward the west, and there shall be a very great valley; and half of the mountain shall be moved toward the north, and half of it toward the south: And you shall flee to the valley of the mountains; for the valley of the mountains shall reach to Azal; yes, you shall flee, like you fled from the earthquake in the days of Uzziah king of Judah; and the L-rd my G-d shall come, and all the holy ones with you: And it shall come to pass on that day, that there shall not be bright light nor thick darkness: But it shall be one day which shall be known to the L-rd, not day, nor night; but it shall come to pass, that at evening time there shall be light: And it shall be on that day, that living waters shall go out from Jerusalem; half of them toward the eastern sea, and half of them toward the western sea; in summer and in winter shall it be: And the L-rd shall be king over all the earth; on that day the L-rd shall be one, and his name one:
>
> Zechariah 14.1-9

Another passage of scripture directly relates to the victory of the Jews over their enemies as the kingdom and the redemption come. This was written by the prophet Malachi.

> For, behold, the day comes, it shall burn like an oven; and all the arrogant, and all who do wickedly, shall be stubble; and the day that comes shall burn them up, says the L-rd of hosts, so that it will not leave them root nor branch: But to you who fear my name the sun of righteousness shall arise with healing in its wings; and you shall go forth leaping like calves from the stall: And you shall trample down the wicked; for they shall be ashes under the soles of your feet on the day that I shall do this, says the L-rd of hosts:
>
> Malachi 3.19-21 (4.1-3)

PROPHECIES IN THE BOOK OF ESTHER

How appropriate that the book of Esther illustrates both the first and second coming of the Messiah. There is yet another fascinating picture of the False Messiah found in these last chapters of Esther. Just as the False Messiah has ten kings that are a part of his empire serving directly under him, so too did Haman have ten sons.

11. The Ten Sons

Haman was hung on the gallows he had constructed for Mordecai immediately following the banquet with Esther and the king. His ten sons, however, were slain at a much later date, the time designated for the slaughter of the Jewish people according to Haman's decree, the 13th of Adar.

Each son's name is listed separately in scripture. Names are listed in scripture to show a special significance, in this case, to show that each son was prominent. In addition, the names of the ten sons are written singly; each on a separate line of text. Usually, when names, or other words, are set apart in Hebrew scripture, they are stacked in the manner of bricks: one whole over two halves, etc. This is not the case with the names of Haman's sons. Their names are written as a whole name over another whole name. This type of stacking in architecture would fail as a sturdy foundation.[1] What is seen by this picture is that although Haman's sons enjoyed power and prosperity, they were easily taken down and defeated.

The Vav

There is another reason why these ten names hold a special significance. Remember that the *Megillah*, the Hebrew scroll of Esther, is written in Hebrew and one character stands differently than the other Hebrew characters in the text. This *vav* is the first character of the last son's name. It also appears larger than the other Hebrew characters making it of special significance.

The rabbis taught that this letter is larger in order to show the

---

[1] (Zlotowitz, 1976, p. 119)

manner of death of the ten sons. The larger *vav*, ו, which resembles a large stake, represents a very large post upon which they believed the 10 sons were impaled on, one above the other,[2] rather than 10 separate gallows.[3]

The term *gallows* can mislead modern readers. The sons and Haman himself were not presumably hung by a noose which is representative of capital punishment in the old west. Instead, the victims of hanging in Persian times were run through a large stake and then left to 'hang' for public exhibition. This then would lend some credence to what the rabbis suspected.

The rabbis speculated another reason the *vav* in the last son's name was illustrated larger was that the *vav* pointed to the sixth millennium.[4] The letter *vav* is the sixth character in the Hebrew

---

[2] (Wikimedia Commons Contributors, 2017)
[3] Ibid.
[4] (Munk, 1983, pp. 94-103)

THE TEN SONS

aleph-bet, and is used for the number six. It also is used to indicate the number of man for having been created on the sixth day. If Adam had not sinned, they would have remained immortal. However, when they sinned, they became subject to death.

The recording of the generations in Genesis also makes a distinction involving the *vav*.

> These are the generations [תוֹלְדוֹת] of the heavens and of the earth when they were created, in the day that the L-rd G-d made the earth and the heavens:
>
> Genesis 2.4

In this verse, the word for "generations" is *toledot* as seen below and the *vav* ו appears twice.

תוֹלְדוֹת (toledot)

However, in all other places, the word is "defective" when one or the other of the *vavim* (pl.), is missing. It is spelled in either one of two ways seen below.

תוֹלְדֹת

or

תֹלְדוֹת

PROPHECIES IN THE BOOK OF ESTHER

Toledot is only fully spelled out in the Hebrew in two verses; Genesis 2.4 and in the following verse from Ruth.

> Now these are the generations [תוֹלְדוֹת] of Perez; Perez fathered Hezron:
>
> Ruth 4.18

This understanding of the significance of the two *vavim* in Ruth 4.18 not only indicates the restoration of man but also that this restoration is accomplished through the work of the Messiah. This can be seen in the song "Lecha Dodi" sung each week as the sun sets on Friday evening to "Welcome the Sabbath". The eighth stanza of this Messianic song reads:

> "Stretch out thy borders to left and to right; Fear but the L-rd, when to fear is delight - The man, son of Perez, shall gladden our sight, And we shall rejoice to the fullness of days..."[5]

When the world was created there was no death, but then Adam sinned.

> "As a result, the "offspring" (*toledoth*) of man are diminished [and this is alluded to by the fact that the word itself is diminished]. But with the coming of the Messiah [who is a descendant of David, who in turn stems from Peretz], then, "Death will be swallowed up forever" (Isaiah 25.8). The "offspring" (*toledoth*) of man will then be complete again, [and for this reason, the genealogy of Peretz is the second place where this word is spelled out in full]."[6]

---

[5] (Hertz D. J., 1948, p. 359)
[6] (Culi, 1979, pp. 277, Vol 1)

THE TEN SONS

The Mishkan - Tabernacle

There is yet another reason why the *vav* is larger within the text of the tenth son listed. This character is used several more times in scripture with special significance. For example, it also relates directly to G-d's tabernacle, the *Mishkan*. The term *vav* means hook and the Hebrew character physically resembles one -

ו

The Radak, in Sefer HaShorashim, explains: "These were pegs [*yataid*] that protruded from the pillars, in the shape of a letter *vav*; they were used to hang the carcasses of the sacrifices when they were being skinned."[7] The courtyard of the *Mishkan* was surrounded by curtains suspended by *vavim* (hooks) from the tops of pillars. Similarly, the rabbis taught that the *vav* is used in scripture to join one thing to another or even one time period to another linking the past to the present and future. The *vav* and the *yataid* both operate as "connectors". The word *vav* is used as a conjunction, connecting people, ideas and times. The *yataid* was used as a hook upon which the Mishkan rested for its structure and function.

The *Mishkan* is the tabernacle itself and has a higher sanctity than the courtyard that surrounds it. As one enters the *Mishkan*, the first room is known as the *haKodesh* or Holy Place. It is in this room that the table of Shewbread, the seven-branched Menorah, and the Altar of Incense stood. A veil separated the *haKodesh* from the next room, the *Kodesh haKodashim*, the Holy of Holies. It was in this room where the Ark of the Covenant was located. A veil separating these two rooms was supported by four vertical poles.

These were not the only vertical poles present within the *Mishkan*. As one entered from the courtyard into the *Mishkan*, going

---

[7] (Leitner, 2007)

into the *haKodesh* there would have been another five poles and a veil suspended from them. The middle pole was known as the *yataid*. This pole was unique in that it had pegs set within.

The vessels of the *Mishkan* were hung on this middle pole, including the measuring cups for the oil of the Menorah. Since this pole was the center pole of the *Mishkan*, the rabbis saw a picture of the Messiah in this singular *yataid* and the sage's further go on to state that the *yataid* of the *Mishkan* was as the anchor of G-d's court. Notice the importance of the *yataid* from this passage in Isaiah.

> Thus said the L-rd G-d of hosts, Go to this steward, to Shebna, who is over the house, and say: What have you here? and whom have you here, that you have cut out for yourself a sepulcher here, as he who cuts out for himself a sepulcher on the height, carving a habitation for himself in a rock: Behold, the L-rd will hurl you away with a mighty throw, and will seize you firmly: He will violently turn and toss you like a ball into a wide land; there shall you die, and there the chariots of your glory shall be the shame of your L-rd's house: And I will drive you from your station, and from your state shall he pull you down:
>
> Isaiah 22.15-19

In the above passage, Sheba holds the position of *Asher al Bayit*, Master of the House. This position was the equivalent to the Prime Minister of the country, second only to the king. He was deposed from his position by G-d and violently overthrown. Following, another character is introduced, Eliakim, who replaces Shebna.

> And it shall come to pass in that day, that I will call my servant Eliakim the son of Hilkiah: And I will clothe him with your robe, and strengthen him with your girdle, and I will commit your government to his hand; and he shall be a father to the inhabitants of Jerusalem, and to the house of Judah: And the key

THE TEN SONS

> of the house of David will I lay upon his shoulder; so he shall open, and none shall close; and he shall close, and none shall open: And I will fasten him as a tent peg [*yataid*] in a sure place; and he shall be for a glorious throne to his father's house:
>
> Isaiah 22.20-23

The Messiah is definitely seen in this passage, and some of these verses are directly applied to Yeshua in the book of Revelation.[8] Notice that G-d states that He will fasten him as a *yataid* in a secure place. For this reason, the *yataid* is a picture of the Messiah. As in the *Mishkan*, all the vessels for the service of the *haKodesh* were hung upon the *yataid*, so will the Father's glory be hung upon the Messiah.

> And they shall hang upon him all the glory of his father's house, the offspring and the issue, all utensils of small quantity, from the utensils of cups, even to all the utensils of flagons:
>
> Isaiah 22.24

The next verse reverts back to Shebna, the one who had been removed from his office. With Eliakim representing the Messiah, then pattern suggests Shebna represents the False Messiah.

> In that day, said the L-rd of hosts, shall the tent peg [*yataid*] that is in the sure place be removed and be cut down, and fall; and the fastened burden that was upon it shall be cut off; for the L-rd has spoken it:
>
> Isaiah 22.25

This prophecy speaks of the future for it says, "In that day," a common reference to the Day of the L-rd. However, the *yataid* referenced in the prophecy is Shebna,[9] a picture of the False Messiah.

---

[8] Revelation 3.7
[9] (Rosenberg, 1982, pp. 102-105)

PROPHECIES IN THE BOOK OF ESTHER

As a result, *yataid* may be used for either the Messiah or the False Messiah. *Yataid*, in this application, symbolizes the ruler of a people.

In the scroll of Esther, the names of the 10 sons are listed singularly in a single column. The rabbi's reason this is related to their importance. It is very likely that following their father's death, these ten sons would have commanded his armies which attacked the Jews.

The last son listed, Vajezatha, ויזתא, begins with the oversized *vav*. It is possible that his name was further distinguished to indicate he was the *yataid* or the leader of the ten. In fact, he may be a direct parallel to Shebna, who is replaced by Eliakim, even as Yeshua will replace the False Messiah.

The Decemviri

Whenever a confederation, group, or alliance of ten men is written in scripture or history, another parallel is hinted at. Soon after the events of Esther had happened, another profound event occurred in another country that may offer insight into the prophetic significance of these ten sons. The story of Esther takes place less than five hundred years before the start of the Common Era. In the same century, on the other side of the Mediterranean Sea, another group of 10 men was meeting. Their actions set in motion consequences that changed the world and its history. Those men were the *Decemviri* from ancient Rome.

Rome was founded and settled about 753 B.C.E. After a few kings, the citizens of the Roman area grew tired of the tyrants who had ruled. This caused the ancient Romans to form a republic. However, a problem persisted for several years, clashes between the two classes of the elite and the common. The patricians were wealthy and powerful while the plebeians were poor and overtaxed. Each group had to serve in the military, but representation from the plebeian caste was restricted to the lower ranks. This led to a series

THE TEN SONS

of disputes between the two classes which lasted many years. During one such dispute, the plebeians withdrew to one of the hills of Rome and settled, insulating themselves from the patricians. These plebeians formed a group known as the Tribunal. At first, the Tribunes were of two men, but the Tribunal later grew to include at least ten. After many more disputes with the patricians, the plebeians urged that a law should be coded for the citizens of Rome, granting equality of sorts to each class. As a result of the patricians relenting, the plebeians commissioned the *Decemviri*, ten men, to write a code of laws that would, ostensibly, protect the rights of all Roman citizens.

Conspicuously, the *Decemviri* were not nobles. They represented a society promising to give legal protection that was much needed. The group formed about 450 B.C.E. and remained for less than two years. The legal code they compiled was called the Twelve Tablets because the codes were written on twelve separate tablets of clay. The actual tablets did not survive, but the laws written on them have survived through the centuries. These laws, developed by the Roman plebeians were among the most complete and complex system of laws in that time of the ancient world. The laws have strongly influenced the character of the laws in virtually every nation of Western Europe, with the exception of England.

Following the fall of the Roman Empire, and through the Middle Ages, the ancient laws fell into disuse. However, late in the Eleventh Century, the ancient Roman laws were rediscovered and studied by scholars. Today, even the United States has been influenced by this old code. For example, the ancient Tribunes had the power to forbid certain action on part of the Roman Senate, comprised of patricians. By calling out, *"Veto"* (I forbid), action could be stopped. Today, the *veto* is a powerful part of the legal system of the United States.

The *Decemviri* provided a service to ancient Rome. However, their corruption and misuse of power forced them from this position less than two years after their commission.

PROPHECIES IN THE BOOK OF ESTHER

We then connect this to the False Messiah as described in Daniel and Revelation who has ten kings directing his empire.

> After this I saw in the night visions, and behold a fourth beast, dreadful and terrible, and exceedingly strong; and it had great iron teeth; it devoured and broke in pieces, and stamped the residue with its feet; and it was different from all the beasts that were before it; and it had ten horns: I considered the horns, and, behold, there came up among them another little horn, before which three of the first horns were plucked up by the roots; and, behold, in this horn were eyes like the eyes of man, and a mouth speaking great things:
>
> Daniel 7.7-8

This passage relates to the rise of the False Messiah over a future revived Roman Empire. The fact that ancient Rome was represented by ten men relates to the ten men under the False Messiah of the future.

> And the ten horns are ten kings that shall arise out of this kingdom, and another shall rise after them; and he shall be different from the former ones, and he shall subdue three kings:
>
> Daniel 7.24

The horns in the preceding passage are defined as ten rulers, the False Messiah rising after them. The book of Revelation uses the same metaphor of the ten crowns to describe the ten rulers subjoined with the False Messiah.

THE TEN SONS

> And I stood upon the sand of the sea, and saw a beast rise up out of the sea, having seven heads and ten horns, and upon his horns ten crowns, and upon his heads the name of blasphemy.
>
> Revelation 13.1

With the revival of the old Roman Empire under the leadership of the False Messiah soon to come, it will be interesting to see if the confederations of ambassadors from the ten nations share characteristics with the *Decemviri* and the sons of Haman...

> And the ten horns which thou sawest are ten kings, which have received no kingdom as yet; but receive power as kings one hour with the beast.
>
> Revelation 17.12

It would be reasonable to believe the sons of Haman, in their effort to carry out their father's wishes to ethnically cleanse the country, portrayed themselves as nationalistic. They were likely leaders and instigators in the campaign to destroy all the Jews in the one hundred twenty-seven provinces, and wipe the Jews from the face of the earth. Similarly, the False Messiah and his ten rulers will seek to "ethnically cleanse" by ridding the world of G-d's people.

What many do not realize from the following verses is that the saints, *Tzaddikim* in Hebrew, are Jews and non-Jews who keep Torah and believe in Yeshua.

> And when the dragon saw that he was cast unto the earth, he persecuted the woman which brought forth the man child. And to the woman were given two wings of a great eagle, that she might fly into the wilderness, into her place, where she is nourished for a time, and times, and half a time, from the face of the serpent. And the serpent cast out of his mouth water as a flood after the woman, that he might cause her to be carried away of the flood. And the earth helped the woman, and the earth opened her

mouth, and swallowed up the flood which the dragon cast out of his mouth. And the dragon was wroth with the woman, and went to make war with the remnant of her seed, which keep the commandments of G-d, and have the testimony of Yeshua the Messiah.

Revelation 12.13-17

In this passage, the woman who flees into the wilderness to a place prepared by G-d is a symbol of the Jewish people. Their flight is during the last three and a half years of the Birthpains of The Messiah (the tribulation). The dragon that sends a flood (army) after them is the False Messiah and his ten rulers. He goes to make war with those of Israel who did not make it into the wilderness. Notice that they are Torah observant and have the testimony of Yeshua the Messiah. They are *Tzaddikim.*

When the Children of Israel were delivered by G-d out of Egypt, this was known as the first redemption. The events of the second coming of the Messiah and the deliverance of the Jewish people are known as the second redemption. As when Israel came out of Egypt, there were many non-Jews known as the mixed multitude that went out with them. These non-Jews were joining themselves to the Jewish people and to their G-d. Caleb was one of these righteous non-Jews.[10]

And a mixed multitude went up also with them; and flocks, and herds, and very many cattle:

Exodus 12.38

During the first century, many non-Jews became believers in the Messiah. In doing this, they joined themselves to Israel, a mixed multitude that went out with them.

These non-Jewish believers were known as the *Yireh*

---

[10] Numbers 32.12; Joshua 14.6,14

THE TEN SONS

Shamayim, the G-d Fearers, and even though they did not become Jewish, they observed the Sabbath, the Biblical Festivals, and ate kosher foods. They renounced all forms of idolatry and accepted the basic tenants of Torah faith which had been given by G-d.

Once again, in the time of the Birthpains of the Messiah, that which happened before will happen again. All of Israel will receive the Messiah.

> For I would not, brethren, that ye should be ignorant of this mystery, lest ye should be wise in your own conceits; that blindness in part is happened to Israel, until the fulness of the Gentiles be come in. And so all Israel shall be saved: as it is written, There shall come out of Sion the Deliverer, and shall turn away ungodliness from Jacob: For this is my covenant unto them, when I shall take away their sins.
>
> Romans 11.25-27

Many non-Jews will also become believers as revealed in the book of Revelation.

> After this I beheld, and, lo, a great multitude, which no man could number, of all nations, and kindreds, and people, and tongues, stood before the throne, and before the Lamb, clothed with white robes, and palms in their hands; And cried with a loud voice, saying, Salvation to our G-d which sitteth upon the throne, and unto the Lamb.
>
> Revelation 7.9-10

Unlike the faith of today, which for most believers is so totally estranged from Torah, the faith during the Birthpains of the Messiah will be returned to its first-century model. These are the believers, or saints, both Jews and non-Jews, against whom the False Messiah makes war, even as Haman and his ten sons made war against the Jews and those who had joined with them.

PROPHECIES IN THE BOOK OF ESTHER

> And it was given unto him to make war with the saints, and to overcome them: and power was given him over all kindreds, and tongues, and nations.
>
> Revelation 13.7

A parallel passage is found in the prophecy of Daniel. From this verse, the *Tzaddikim*, possess the Kingdom with the coming of the Messiah, even as in Haman's day the Jews were triumphant in the kingdom.

> As I looked the same horn made war with the holy ones, and prevailed against them: Until the ancient of days came, and judgment was given for the holy ones of the most High; and the time came that the holy ones possessed the kingdom:
>
> Daniel 7.21-22

In the same manner the ten sons of Haman unitedly served their father, likewise, the leaders of the future ten nations will submit all their authority and power to the False Messiah.

> These have one mind, and shall give their power and strength unto the beast.
>
> Revelation 17.13

Comparable to the Decemviri, who were responsible for putting into place prominent and influential new laws, so too will the leaders of the revived Roman Empire reveal their intentions. In the last days, these ten nations will impose legislation changing times and laws not only against G-d's people but against G-d Himself.

> And he shall speak great words against the most High, and shall wear out the holy ones of the most High, and shall think to change the times and the law; and they shall be given into his hand for a time, times and half a time:
>
> Daniel 7.25

THE TEN SONS

World War II

Possibly the most unusual prophecy yet discovered in scripture is the passage about the slaying of Haman's ten sons.

> And in Shushan the capital the Jews slew and destroyed five hundred men: And Parshandatha, and Dalphon, and Aspatha: And Poratha, and Adalia, and Aridatha: And Parmashta, and Arisai, and Aridai, and Vajezatha: The ten sons of Haman the son of Hammedatha, the enemy of the Jews, slew they; but on the plunder they did not lay their hand:
>
> Esther 9.6-10

The events listed above take place on the 13th of Adar with an initial victory over the 10 sons of Haman and the forces they led. Besides the armies they commanded outside of Shushan, 500 men were slain in the capital, including the 10 sons. Once again, the 10 sons were slain on the 13th of Adar.

> On that day the number of those who were slain in Shushan the capital was brought before the king: And the king said to Esther the queen, The Jews have slain and destroyed five hundred men in Shushan the capital, and the ten sons of Haman; what have they done in the rest of the king's provinces? now what is your petition? and it shall be granted you; or what is your request further? and it shall be done:
>
> Esther 9.11-12

In the above passage, the king acknowledged the deaths of the 500 men in Shushan as well as the death of the 10 sons of Haman. He inquired of the results of the war throughout the rest of the empire. Then he asked Esther what further request she might have. Her answer has raised many questions over the years.

PROPHECIES IN THE BOOK OF ESTHER

> Then said Esther, If it please the king, let it be granted to the Jews who are in Shushan to do tomorrow also according to this day's decree, and let Haman's ten sons be hanged upon the gallows: And the king commanded it so to be done; and the decree was given at Shushan; and they hanged Haman's ten sons:
>
> Esther 9.13-14

First, she requests that on the 14th of Adar, the Jews in Shushan be allowed to continue the war on the anti-Semitic forces for one more day. She further requested that Haman's 10 sons be hanged, or in this case, impaled upon a stake for public view. What is strange about this is that they were slain in the previous day's battle. Why slay them twice? For centuries this question has baffled scholars and is the cause of much speculation.

During World War II, the Nazis of Germany under Hitler followed the same path as Haman. The Nazi dictator Hitler banned and forbade the observance of Purim. On November 10, 1938, the day after Kristallnacht, Julius Streicher made a spurious speech against the Jews. Streicher, head of the Nazi Party in Nuremberg stated that "the Jews butchered 75,000 Persians" in one night, conveniently leaving out the king's decree for self-defense. Streicher declared that had the Jews succeeded in inciting a war against Germany, the same fate would befall the German people and "Jews would have instituted a new Purim festival in Germany."[11]

This resulted in numerous attacks against the Jews. These acts of violence were committed during Purim such as the hanging of ten Jews, in Zduńska Wola, Poland in 1942.[12] The following year on Purim, 10 Jews from the Piotrków Trybunalski Ghetto, were also shot. On Purim eve that same year, over 100 Jewish doctors and their families were shot in Częstochowa, Poland. The following day

---

[11] (Bytwerk, 2008, p. 91)
[12] (Cohen, 2009, p. 948)

THE TEN SONS

Jewish doctors were taken from Radom and shot in Szydłowiec in southeastern Poland.[13]

Hitler too identified with Haman in a speech given January 30, 1944, saying that if the Nazis were defeated, the Jews could celebrate "a second Purim".[14]

The Nuremberg Trials

Following the end of the war, high ranking Nazis were tried in Nuremberg, Germany for various war crimes. They had tried to obliterate the Jews from the face of the earth. When the war came to an end in 1945, the surviving top Nazi officers were tried for war crimes at the infamous Nuremberg War Trials. At the top of the list for war crimes was involvement in the holocaust, in which 6 million Jews and several million others were torturously put to their deaths. At the conclusion of the trial, 11 men were given the death penalty by hanging. What is remarkable about this ruling is that the standard method of execution in a military trial is death by a firing squad. The date set for their hanging was October 16th, 1946. Just two hours before the scheduled execution, Hermann Goering, one of the convicted 11 committed suicide by ingesting cyanide poison. This left 10 men to be executed.

One of the 10 was Julius Streicher who on the gallows just prior to his death, "with burning hatred in his eyes ... looked down at the witnesses and shouted: 'Purim Fest 1946.'"[15] He then shouted, "Heil Hitler," as the floor gave way beneath him.

Streicher had been a Nazi since early on in the movement and

---

[13] (Horowitz, 2006, p. 91)
[14] Ibid.
[15] (Smith, 1946) (Wistrich, 1995, p. 252), "The Jewish holiday Purim celebrates the escape by the Jews from extermination at the hands of Haman, an ancient Persian government official. At the end of the Purim story, Haman is hanged, as are his ten sons." (October 28, 1946). (Rubin, 2011)

PROPHECIES IN THE BOOK OF ESTHER

had offices in Nuremberg, a center for Nazis. He was the editor and publisher of the anti-Semitic newspaper, *"Der Stürmer."* In May of 1924, Streicher wrote and published an article on Purim titled *"Das Purimfest"* (The Festival of Purim). His article slandered the Jews and was intentionally a part of Nazi propaganda preceding and during the holocaust. It is clear Streicher was familiar with the festival, but why would his dying words be "Purim Fest 1946?"

The answer is quite astounding. In the list of the names of Haman's 10 sons, there are several Hebrew letters that are written in a most unusual fashion. Earlier, the enlarged *vav* ו, was addressed but we find there is more. In three of the son's names, one Hebrew character in each name is noticeably smaller than the surrounding characters. These undersized letters are found in the names of the first, seventh, and tenth son. The first is, *Parshandatha,* spelled

פרשנדתא

Notice that the *tav*, ת is undersized. This is all the more remarkable when we recall that the words and letters were written by divine inspiration of the Holy Spirit.[16] The next undersized letter is found in the name, *Parmashta,* the seventh son of Haman. His name is spelled

פרמשתא

In this name, the undersized letter is the *shin,* ש. The third and final small letter is discovered in Haman's 10th son, *Vajezatha.* In Hebrew, his name is spelled

ויזתא

The undersized letter here is the *zayin* ז.

---

[16] 2 Timothy 3.16-17

THE TEN SONS

Sons of Haman	
וְאֵת	אִישׁ
וְאֵת	פַּרְשַׁנְדָּ֨תָא
וְאֵת	דַּלְפוֹן
וְאֵת	אַסְפָּתָא
וְאֵת	פּוֹרָתָא
וְאֵת	אֲדַלְיָא
וְאֵת	אֲרִידָתָא
וְאֵת	פַּרְמַ֨שְׁתָּא
וְאֵת	אֲרִיסַי
וְאֵת	אֲרִידַי
עֲשֶׂרֶת	וַ֨יְזָתָא

The Hebrew alphabet is used to represent numbers as well. When the numeric value of these three letters are added up according to their given values of 400 = ת, 300 = שׁ, 7 = ז they total 707.

$$\begin{array}{rr} ת & 400 \\ שׁ & 300 \\ ז & 7 \\ \hline & 707 \end{array}$$

Adding 5000 years for the sixth millennium[17] represented by the enlarged *vav* ו adds up to the Jewish year 5707, which was according to the Roman calendar, 1946. Astonishingly, the Nuremberg hangings took place in 1946. Additionally, the execution took place on October 16th, which on the Hebrew calendar for that year was the 21st of *Tishri*, the first month of the Hebrew civil calendar.

---

[17] The sixth millennium is the period between years 5000 to 6000 on the Jewish calendar.

PROPHECIES IN THE BOOK OF ESTHER

ה'תש"ז (5707) 1946-47

SEP - OCT   תשרי

ראשון SUN	שני MON	שלישי TUE	רביעי WED	חמישי THU	ששי FRI	שבת SAT
—	—	—	—	א / 26	ב / 27	ג / 28
ז / 29	ה / 30	ו / 1	ז / 2	ח / 3	ט / 4	י / 5
יא / 6	יב / 7	יג / 8	יד / 9	טו / 10	טז / 11	יז / 12
יח / 13	ית / 14	כ / 15	(כא / 16)	כב / 17	כג / 18	כד / 19
כה / 20	כו / 21	כז / 22	כח / 23	כת / 24	ל / 25	—

Judged, Sealed and Executed

There are three festivals prescribed by G-d in Leviticus 23 that take place in the month of *Tishri: Rosh Hashanah,* the first day of the month, *Yom Kippur,* the tenth day, and *Sukkot,* a festival of seven days from the 15th until the 21st. Two other names for *Rosh Hashanah* include *Yom haDin,* the Day of Judgment, and *Yom haTeruah,* the Day of the Awakening Blast. *Yom Kippur* is the Day of Atonement. *Sukkot,* the Festival of Booths or Tabernacles, ends with *Hoshana Rabba,* the Great Salvation. A well-known teaching from the Talmud *Yerushalami* (Jerusalem)[18] tractate *Rosh Hashanah*[19] is that "man is judged on *Rosh Hashanah,* sealed on *Yom Kippur,* and executed on *Hoshana Rabbah.*"[20] In this same section of the Talmud, there is yet more that points to the Nuremberg hangings.

---

[18] The *Talmud* is an expansion and commentary of the Oral Torah.
[19] A section of the *Talmud* that comments on the festival of *Rosh haShanah.*
[20] Yerushalami Rosh haShanah 84.8

THE TEN SONS

Following each of Haman's son's names, there is a Hebrew word.

$$V'et - \text{ואת}$$

This is a grammatically non-translated word. The word *V'et* points to an article coming up in the next word; however, it also has another meaning – "there are ten more." What has been expounded from this is that in addition to the ten sons of Haman, "there are ten more," as in the Nuremberg Ten, who were of the spirit of Haman and his sons.

What if these encoded messages concealed why the ten sons of Haman were hung after they had previously been slain? Earlier in the chapter relating the death of Haman, it was stated that whoever is hung on a tree is cursed.[21] Though the Messiah was hung and thought to be cursed, He was lifted up as a sign of His complete innocence. But the ten men in the book of Esther and the Nuremberg ten, guilty for warring against G-d and His people, received divine justice as will the cursed False Messiah and his ten.

A very important point to remember is that all of these events in the days of Esther and Mordecai, as well as the executions of the Nazis, are forerunners of the coming False Messiah and his ten men. These are previews of their final end.

> That which has been, is what shall be; and that which has been done is what shall be done; and there is nothing new under the sun:
>
> Ecclesiastes 1.9

---

[21] Deuteronomy 21.22-23

PROPHECIES IN THE BOOK OF ESTHER

The False Messiah and the Ten Leaders

The initial battle against the enemies of the Jews was accomplished on the 13th of Adar; however, in Shushan, the capital of the Persian Empire, Esther requested permission for the Jews to have an additional day to thoroughly annihilate the enemies of her people.

> For the Jews who were in Shushan gathered themselves together also on the fourteenth day of the month Adar, and slew three hundred men at Shushan; but on the plunder they did not lay their hand: But the other Jews who were in the king's provinces gathered themselves together, and stood for their lives, and had rest from their enemies, and slew of their foes seventy five thousand, but they laid not their hands on the plunder:
>
> Esther 9.15-16

This is exactly in accord with what is recorded in the balance of scriptures. There will be the battle against the False Messiah and his forces when Yeshua returns, which relates to the battles of the 13th and 14th of Adar.

THE TEN SONS

And I saw heaven opened, and behold a white horse; and he that sat upon him was called Faithful and True, and in righteousness he doth judge and make war. His eyes were as a flame of fire, and on his head were many crowns; and he had a name written, that no man knew, but he himself. And he was clothed with a vesture dipped in blood: and his name is called The Word of G-d. And the armies which were in heaven followed him upon white horses, clothed in fine linen, white and clean. And out of his mouth goeth a sharp sword, that with it he should smite the nations: and he shall rule them with a rod of iron: and he treadeth the winepress of the fierceness and wrath of Almighty G-d. And he hath on his vesture and on his thigh a name written, KING OF KINGS, AND LORD OF LORDS. And I saw an angel standing in the sun; and he cried with a loud voice, saying to all the fowls that fly in the midst of heaven, Come and gather yourselves together unto the supper of the great G-d; That ye may eat the flesh of kings, and the flesh of captains, and the flesh of mighty men, and the flesh of horses, and of them that sit on them, and the flesh of all men, both free and bond, both small and great. And I saw the beast, and the kings of the earth, and their armies, gathered together to make war against him that sat on the horse, and against his army. And the beast was taken, and with him the false prophet that wrought miracles before him, with which he deceived them that had received the mark of the beast, and them that worshipped his image. These both were cast alive into a lake of fire burning with brimstone. And the remnant were slain with the sword of him that sat upon the horse, which sword proceeded out of his mouth: and all the fowls were filled with their flesh.

Revelation 19.11-21

PROPHECIES IN THE BOOK OF ESTHER

Adar 13 – 1000 Years Later – Adar 14

Why are there two days in the book of Esther in which the Jews fight their enemies? In the book of Esther on Adar 13, the enemies hoped to have power over the Jews[22] but instead, it was the Jews who were "gathered together" in such a way that no man could withstand them and they smote all their enemies with the stroke of the sword.[23]

This day, Adar 13, is a picture of the Messiah's return at the start of the seventh millennium. On Adar 13, there is a victory over the enemies of the Jews as portrayed by the king, Esther and Mordecai. This battle, which occurred in Shushan, pictures one of the battles to come in the last days, but this time in Jerusalem, the residence of the true King. Shushan, as one of the capitals of the Persian Empire, in this context symbolizes Jerusalem, the capital of the world.[24]

Jerusalem is where Yeshua and His bride will be together in the battle for victory. It's only after the king's scepter first gives Esther permission to enter his domain that the three of them, the king, Esther, and Mordecai, start to act together as one. The moment the king grants Esther her life and up to half his kingdom, both Esther and Mordecai begin to jointly act with the king's authority.[25]

This day is a picture of the first judgment that occurs after the first battle at the Messiah's coming. Riding on a white horse as King of kings with a sharp sword, the Messiah casts the beast, symbolized both by the ten nations and the ten sons, along with the false messiah depicted by Haman, into the lake of fire.[26] This is the first judgment.

---

[22] Esther 9.1
[23] Esther 9.2,5
[24] Jeremiah 17.12; Ezekiel 43.6-7
[25] Esther 8.8
[26] Revelation 19.20

THE TEN SONS

> For a thousand years in thy sight *are but* as yesterday when it is past, and *as* a watch in the night.
>
> Psalms 90.4 KJV

The following day on Adar 14, in the book of Esther, a second decisive battle took place. In this battle once again the Jews gathered together to defend themselves. They solely fought to preserve their lives and did not take any of the spoils to themselves. Many not only joined in the battle but also became Jews because the "fear of the Jews came upon them."

> There shall no man be able to stand before you: *for* the L-RD your G-d shall lay the fear of you and the dread of you upon all the land that ye shall tread upon, as he hath said unto you.
>
> Deuteronomy 11.25 KJV

The enemies that came hatefully against the Jews were slaughtered; all those who allied with the Amalekites were completely destroyed. In this manner, the remembrance of Amalek was figuratively put out from the kingdom.

> And the L-RD said unto Moses, Write this *for* a memorial in a book, and rehearse *it* in the ears of Joshua: for I will utterly put out the remembrance of Amalek from under heaven.
>
> Exodus 17.14 KJV

In parallel, the second and final battle occurs at the end of the Messiah's thousand year reign.

> But, beloved, be not ignorant of this one thing, that one day *is* with the L-rd as a thousand years, and a thousand years as one day. The L-rd is not slack concerning his promise, as some men count slackness; but is longsuffering to us-ward, not willing

PROPHECIES IN THE BOOK OF ESTHER

> that any should perish, but that all should come to repentance. But the day of the L-rd will come as a thief in the night; in the which the heavens shall pass away with a great noise, and the elements shall melt with fervent heat, the earth also and the works that are therein shall be burned up.
>
> 2 Peter 3.8-10 KJV

The second battle in the book of Esther is representative of the final battle that occurs after the 1,000 year reign of the Messiah. The second and final judgment occurs at this time, the White Throne Judgement.

> And I saw a great white throne, and him that sat on it, from whose face the earth and the heaven fled away; and there was found no place for them.
>
> Revelation 20.11 KJV

During this final battle at the end of the millennium, the last of the enemies of G-d and His people are revealed and finally, utterly destroyed. Though they've had a thousand years, as a day, to repent, turn and join with the Children of Israel, they choose instead to fight against the King Himself. In the final battle, they prefer the edict of the now dead false messiah and are led by Satan.

> And shall go out to deceive the nations which are in the four quarters of the earth, Gog and Magog, to gather them together to battle: the number of whom *is* as the sand of the sea. And they went up on the breadth of the earth, and compassed the camp of the saints about, and the beloved city: and fire came down from G-d out of heaven, and devoured them.
>
> Revelation 20.8-9 KJV

During this final judgment, aside from those who were a part of the first resurrection, the remainder who have ever lived and died will take part in the second resurrection.

THE TEN SONS

And I saw the dead, small and great, stand before G-d; and the books were opened: and another book was opened, which is *the book* of life: and the dead were judged out of those things which were written in the books, according to their works. And the sea gave up the dead which were in it; and death and hell delivered up the dead which were in them: and they were judged every man according to their works.
>Revelation 20.12-13 KJV

The sheep are the believers who go into the Kingdom, whereas the goats are those who have rejected the Messiah.

And death and hell were cast into the lake of fire. This is the second death. And whosoever was not found written in the book of life was cast into the lake of fire.
>Revelation 20.14-15 KJV

At the end of both battles, there is rest, feasting and joy. Just as Purim was celebrated in the days of Esther, so too will the saints have light, gladness, joy and honor.[27]

A Psalm of David. The L-RD *is* my light and my salvation; whom shall I fear? the L-RD *is* the strength of my life; of whom shall I be afraid?
>Psalms 27.1 KJV

O house of Jacob, come ye, and let us walk in the light of the L-RD.
>Isaiah 2.5 KJV

---

[27] Esther 8:16

PROPHECIES IN THE BOOK OF ESTHER

12. Purim

For more than twenty-five hundred years, Jews around the world have celebrated the festival of Purim in remembrance of the defeat of Haman, his ten sons, and anti-Semites. Purim is one of the most enjoyable days of the year throughout Jewry celebrating salvation and deliverance from their enemies.

> But the Jews who were at Shushan assembled together on the thirteenth day of the month, and on the fourteenth day; and on the fifteenth day of the same they rested, and made it a day of feasting and gladness: Therefore the Jews of the villages, who lived in the unwalled towns, make the fourteenth day of the month Adar a day of gladness and feasting, and a holiday, and of sending portions one to another:
>
> Esther 9.18-19

The above verses are an expansion of Esther 9.6 and 9.15 where the Jews of Shushan fought on Adar 13 and Adar 14. On Adar 15 they gained relief from their enemies and began to celebrate. The term "unwalled towns" literally means unfortified cities.

> And Mordecai wrote these things, and sent letters to all the Jews that were in all the provinces of the king Ahasuerus, both near and far: To establish this among them, that they should keep the fourteenth day of the month Adar, and the fifteenth day of the same, yearly: Like the days when the Jews rested from their enemies, and the month which was turned

PROPHECIES IN THE BOOK OF ESTHER

to them from sorrow to joy, and from mourning to a holiday; that they should make them days of feasting and joy, and of sending portions one to another, and gifts to the poor:

Esther 9.20-22

From this point, Mordecai established these days to be annual days of celebration. The literal Hebrew states that the days are celebrated from year to year. The rabbis drew from this that these days would continue to be observed even after the coming of the Messiah to establish His earthly kingdom. Another observation of the ancient sages is that the celebration was not to commemorate the downfall of their enemies, but rather to memorialize their salvation and redemption. From the above verse the custom of *Mishloach Manot,* sending of gifts one to another, became a part of the celebration. This gift was interpreted by the rabbis to be only what is edible or drinkable without further preparation. A gift must also consist of two portions. Also, because the term from Esther means 'sending of gifts,' it is preferable to have one's gift delivered by a messenger. *Mishloach Manot* is performed on the day of Purim. In addition, the passage dictates giving gifts to the poor. These gifts are to be of value to the person who receives them and should be given before Purim so that they might be used by the recipient in their celebration of the festival.

Therefore They Called These Days Purim

And the Jews undertook to do as they had begun, and as Mordecai had written to them: Because Haman the son of Hammedatha, the Agagite, the enemy of all the Jews, had plotted against the Jews to destroy them, and had cast Pur, that is, the lot, to consume them, and to destroy them: But when Esther came before the king, he commanded by letters that his wicked plot, which he devised against the Jews, should return upon his own head, and that

PURIM

> he and his sons should be hanged on the gallows: Therefore they called these days Purim after the name of Pur;
>
> Esther 9.23-26a

From the text of the passage above, at first glance, it appears obvious that Purim received its name from the 'lots' that Haman cast to select the day of the Jews destruction. However, on closer examination, a second and more significant reason emerges revealing the heart of the story of Esther and the festival of Purim.[1] While the first reason is the casting of the 'lots' by Haman, the second is described in what follows:

> But when Esther came before the king, he [the king] commanded by letters that his [Haman] wicked plot, which he [Haman] devised against the Jews, should return upon his [Haman] own head, and that he [Haman] and his sons should be hanged on the gallows: Therefore they called these days Purim after the name of Pur;
>
> Esther 9.25-26a

Like so much in the book of Esther, the confirmation that there is a second reason for the name Purim is hidden from plain view, nevertheless, it is profoundly evidenced by scripture as we shall see. Earlier in the book, the day the decree came forward from Ahasuerus that on the fourteenth of Adar the Jews were to be slain, Mordechai donning sackcloth and ashes, positions himself outside the palace gate. As soon as Esther learned of this, she sent an inquiry through a messenger to find out what was going on. Mordecai informed Esther of the crisis and called upon her to act. At first, Esther explained that she could not approach the king without a summons. The penalty for approaching was death unless he chose to hold out his golden

---

[1] This information comes from *The Queen You Thought You Knew*. For a fuller study of this material, please refer to Rabbi Fohrman's book. (Fohrman, 2011)

scepter. Mordechai sends a second message to Esther that convinced her to approach the king. The exact wording of Mordecai's words is very significant.

> "If you keep silent at this time, salvation will come to the Jews from somewhere else, and you and your father's house will be destroyed. And who knows if it was for this moment that you became queen?
>
> Esther 4.14[2]

To begin with, the statement that she must react, not because the salvation of the Jews depended upon her, but rather, that she and her house would be destroyed if she did not respond personally, seems out of context from what would have been expected. It seems that the text should read:

> *"If you keep silent at this time, destruction will come to the Jews, destroying you and your father's house in the process. Only you can deliver the people. And who knows if it was for this moment that you became queen?*

There seems to be a hidden message in Mordechai's words that Esther would understand. In order to decipher that message, observe what Mordechai wrote as translated directly and literally from Hebrew. Mordechai told Esther she could not remain silent. The Hebrew verb used here for "silent" is *lehacharish*. This verb not only means to "be silent" but also "to be deaf" to what was said. Also, in this passage the verb is doubled:

Im hacharesh tacharishi...

Occasionally a verb is repeated twice in a row in Hebrew and usually serves to emphasize a point. In English it should be translated:

---

[2] In this section the scriptures quoted in English are from Rabbi Fohrman's literal translations. (Fohrman, 2011)

PURIM

If you keep completely silent...

There is only one other place in the *Tanach* where this verb is doubled:

> Any vow or restrictive oath that would cause hardship, her husband can affirm [the vow] or the husband can annul it. [But] if the husband is silent, yes silent (*V'im hacharesh yicharish*), from day to day – then he will have affirmed all her vows or restrictions. He has affirmed them, for he has been silent on the day he heard of it. And if [the husband] [later tries to] annul [her vow] after he [first] heard of it [and was silent], he bears her sin...These are the laws of a *na'arah* [young maiden]...in her father's house.
> Numbers 30.13-15(16)[3]

This double usage of the verb *lehacharish* is in the context of the law pertaining to a young maiden (*na'arah*) in her father's house or a young married woman in her husband's house who has made a vow, and her father or husband's authorization to annul that vow.

Notice that there is a time limit on how long the man had within which to respond. This was only necessary if he intended to annul her vow. He could verbally affirm the vow or simply wait past the day he heard of the vow whereas it would automatically be affirmed. There is a problem with the affirmation option. If the *na'arah* takes a vow and it is affirmed either by verbal affirmation or deafness by her father or husband then the vow stands. He must act on the day he hears it, afterward, her husband can no longer annul it. But if he does change his mind about it and seeks to annul her unfulfilled vow, then he becomes the bearer of the sin and the consequences of the vow.

---

[3] Ibid.

PROPHECIES IN THE BOOK OF ESTHER

A question that might be raised is how does this apply to Esther? Mordecai's urgent reply to Esther is actually saturated with language borrowed from the above passage. Esther is called several times within the text of the *Megillah* (Scroll of Esther) a *na'arah*,[4] a young woman within her father's household or a young married woman under her husband's roof. Even though Esther was the *na'arah*, she's instructed by Mordecai to act in the place of a אִישָׁה (ishah) upon hearing her husband's vow. She is counseled "not to remain silent."

Rabbi David Fohrman makes an interesting observation regarding the Hebrew word used for "husband." The word is transliterated into English as *"ishah."* Examining the phrase of Numbers 31.13 in English, it reads:

"*...her husband can affirm [the vow] or the husband can annul it.*"

In Hebrew, this reads as:

"***ishah** yekimenah, v'**ishah** yepheiremah.*"

What is unique about the Hebrew word "ishah"

אִישָׁה

spelled *aleph, yud, shin, hei* is that the *hei* has a *dagesh* or dot within it serving as a vowel. The word *"ish"* means *"man,"* whereas the feminine form of the word is *ishah is* "woman", in Hebrew it is

אִשָּׁה

The dagesh or dot placed within the *hei* makes the word

---

[4] Esther is described within the *Megillah* as a *na'arah*, a girl on the cusp of adulthood. Esther 2:2-4, 7-9, 12-13; 4:4, 16

PURIM

possessive and expresses as "her ish" or husband. It is important to recall that the Hebrew text was anciently written without any vowels and is still preserved this way when reading from a scroll.

By removing the *dagesh* from the *hei,* the passage would now translate:

A woman can affirm; a woman can annul...

With the above understanding, the passage from Numbers 30 would immediately apply directly to Esther and explain the words of Mordechai.[5] King Ahasuerus has made a verbal declaration that will bring destruction to the Jewish people. Esther, as his wife, can protest his decree, thereby negating it.

---

[5] Rabbi Forhman included the following note explaining his position on his research. Since I have based this material on that research and conclusions I am including his entire statement: "I do not mean to imply a *legal* or *halachic,* equivalence between Esther and the *na'arah* described in the Book of Numbers, or, for that matter, between Esther and that *na'arah's* husband. According to the Book of Numbers, the prerogative to annul vows belongs to a husband. Moreover, in issuing an edict to destroy the Jews, the king has not, in the strict sense of the word, taken a vow. Hence, in a legal sense, the passage in Numbers does not apply to Esther's case. Nevertheless, by overtly interpolating language from the Book of Numbers into Mordechai's words to Esther, the Megillah seems to be suggesting a conceptual, if not a legal, equivalence between the situations. Esther, like the husband in the Book of Numbers, has both the power and the responsibility to respond to an impetuous declaration made by a spouse. She, like he, can protest in delivering that declaration from the realm of potentiality into reality. If she chooses the latter path, she, like the husband in the Book of Numbers, will bear responsibility for that declaration, whether she likes it or not."

PROPHECIES IN THE BOOK OF ESTHER

The Two Reasons the Festival is Called Purim

The proof that Numbers 30 serves as the background of Mordecai's message to Esther and also the theme of the entire book is confirmed by the Hebrew word for annulling a vow. Below is Rabbi Forhman's explanation.

> As it turns out, the word the Book of Numbers uses for "annulling" the declaration of one's spouse – *yepheirena* – just happens to derive from the word *pur*, the word which in Ancient Persian or Aramaic means lots, just happens, in Biblical Hebrew, to mean: "annul."[6]

Indeed, the first reason the festival is called *Purim* was due to the *lots*:

> Because Haman the son of Hammedatha, the Agagite, the enemy of all the Jews, had plotted against the Jews to destroy them, and had cast Pur, that is, the lot, to consume them, and to destroy them:
>
> Esther 9.24

While the second reason the festival is called Purim reflects that Esther made King Ahasuerus's decree as null or ineffective:

> But when Esther came before the king, he commanded by letters that his wicked plot, which he devised against the Jews, should return upon his

---

[6] (Fohrman, 2011, p. 118) "According to the medieval dictionary of roots, *Sefer HaShorashim*, by Rabbi David Kimchi, the root for the Biblical word *annul*, as found in the Book of Numbers, is in fact *peh, vav, reish* – the very letters that spell *pur*."

PURIM

own head, and that he and his sons should be hanged on the gallows: Therefore they called these days Purim after the name of Pur;

Esther 9.25-26a

The Institution of Purim

Therefore for all the words of this letter, and of that which they had seen concerning this matter, and which had come to them: The Jews ordained, and took upon them, and upon their seed, and upon all who joined themselves to them, so as it should not fail, that they would keep these two days according to their writing, and according to their appointed time every year: And that these days should be remembered and kept throughout every generation, every family, every province, and every city; and that these days of Purim should not fail from among the Jews, nor the memorial of them perish from their seed:

Esther 9.26b-28

The above passage was noted by the rabbis as being one of the most important from the book of Esther with many hidden meanings of profound significance. According to Hebrew grammar, when using a plural noun such as 'Jews,' a plural verb is required. However, this passage begins, "And the Jews (plural) undertook (singular)" using the Hebrew singular verb *kevail*, which literally means "he (singular) accepted." A unity developed in which all the Jewish people throughout the world became as one in accepting the obligation to observe this festival throughout their generations. This action is a reflection of when G-d gave the written Torah at Mount Sinai.

PROPHECIES IN THE BOOK OF ESTHER

> For they had departed from Rephidim, and had come to the desert of Sinai, and had camped in the wilderness; and there Israel camped before the mount:
>
> Exodus 19.2

    Israel (plural noun) camped (singular verb) as one before G-d rather than as a nation of individuals. This was necessary in order for Israel to receive G-d's Torah. This passage was also interpreted as a prophecy of when Messiah would come and establish the Holy Kingdom on earth, for in that day the entire earth will be under the kingship of G-d.

> And the L-rd shall be king over all the earth; on that day the L-rd shall be one, and his name one:
>
> Zechariah 14.9

    This is how the receiving of the festival of Purim is equated to the Jews receiving the Torah at Mount Sinai. It is noted that just as the first acceptance of the Torah followed a victorious war with Amalek; here also the war with Amalek's descendant, Haman, was followed by a re-acceptance of the Torah.[7] In this same manner, all of Israel will turn back to G-d and follow His Torah as Messiah comes in the final redemption.[8]

    The festival received its name from Mordecai who named it after the 'lots,' *Purim,* that Haman cast to determine which day to annihilate the Jews. The decree of Ahasuerus, which returned Haman's wicked scheme back onto his own head and sent him and his ten sons to the gallows, is an eternal message to all. To strive against Israel is to strive against G-d. The Holy one has decreed that Israel cannot be destroyed,

---

[7] (Tokayer, 2011)
[8] Romans 10.25; Isaiah 59.20-21; Sanhedrin 10.1

PURIM

> Thus says the L-rd, who gives the sun for a light by day, and the fixed order of the moon and of the stars for a light by night, which divides the sea when its waves roar; The L-rd of hosts is his name: If those ordinances depart from before me, says the L-rd, then the seed of Israel also shall cease from being a nation before me for ever: Thus says the L-rd; If heaven above can be measured, and the foundations of the earth explored below, then I will also cast off all the seed of Israel for all that they have done, says the L-rd: Behold, the days come, says the L-rd, when the city shall be built to the L-rd from the Tower of Hananeel to the Corner's Gate: And the measuring line shall go further straight to the hill Gareb, and shall turn around to go to Goath: And the whole valley of the dead bodies, and of the ashes, and all the fields as far as the brook of Kidron, to the corner of the Horse Gate toward the east, shall be holy to the L-rd; it shall not be plucked up, nor pulled down any more for ever:
>
> Jeremiah 31.34-39 (31.35-40)

History is littered with examples of nations and peoples who have come against Israel resulting in themselves being destroyed. Likewise, this will be the end of the False Messiah and of Satan.

It is significant that the people agreed to "keep these days according to their writing." The understanding of this is the definition of how one is to observe the festival of Purim. Earlier it was stated that these were days of feasting and gladness. This was interpreted to mean eating and drinking and merry-making. During the festival, it is the custom to wear costumes, in particular, those that relate to the story of Esther, even though this is not required. During the Purim parties, there are many skits to remember the desperate situation the Jewish people found themselves in due to Haman and to commemorate G-d's miraculous delivery.

PROPHECIES IN THE BOOK OF ESTHER

"These days should be remembered," is interpreted as the command for the reading of the *Megillah* on this day. During the reading, which is to be done in a light and humorous manner, and consistent with the joy of the festival, the name Haman is to be drowned out when read. This is accomplished by any number of noise-makers. The festival of Purim is indeed one of the most joyous days of the year.

> Then Esther the queen, the daughter of Abihail, and Mordecai the Jew, wrote with all authority, to confirm this second letter of Purim: And he sent the letters to all the Jews, to the one hundred and twenty seven provinces of the kingdom of Ahasuerus, in words of peace and truth: To confirm these days of Purim in their times appointed, according as Mordecai the Jew and Esther the queen had enjoined them, and as they had decreed for themselves and for their seed, with regard to the fasting and their lamenting: And the decree of Esther confirmed these matters of Purim; and it was written in the book:

> Esther 9.29-32

This second letter written by Esther and sent by Mordecai throughout the kingdom ends with words of peace and truth. This was understood to be the conclusion of the book even though there are three more verses. These verses are profound as they underline one of the major themes of the book of Esther, the rebuilding of the Temple. Earlier it was stated that the Jewish view of Haman's motives for his evil scheme was to destroy the rebuilding of the Holy Temple in Jerusalem. The resulting peace and truth would ensure the rebuilding of the Temple.

> And the king Ahasuerus laid a tribute upon the land, and upon the islands of the sea: And all the acts of his power and of his might, and the declaration of the greatness of Mordecai, to which the king advanced him, are they not written in the Book of the

PURIM

Chronicles of the kings of Media and Persia: For Mordecai the Jew was next to king Ahasuerus, and great among the Jews, and accepted by the multitude of his brothers, seeking the good of his people, and speaking peace to all his seed:

Esther 10.1-3

The closing verses of Esther give a concise and accurate picture of Yeshua the Messiah and the state of the kingdom on earth after His return. There will be a time of prosperity and peace, a time when the Holy Temple will be rebuilt, and all the earth will be under the Kingship of G-d.

The book of Esther and the festival of Purim are delights in scripture as they teach that righteousness triumphs over evil. The story of Esther serves as an encouragement to exhibit faith in the hand of G-d working behind the scene to accomplish His plans and bring all into a complete peace. It also comments on the severity of the crimes of anti-Semitism and those who seek to destroy the people of G-d. There is much richness and blessings in the book of Esther encouraging us as we wait for the Messiah to return.

Blessed are You, L-rd our G-d, King of the Universe, who pleads our cause, judges our claim, avenges our wrong, brings retribution to our enemies, and punishes our foes. Blessed are You, L-rd, who on behalf of His people Israel, exacts punishment from all their foes, the G-d who brings salvation.[9]

---

[9] (Sacks, 2015, p. 902) This is read following the reading and rolling of the Esther scroll when a minyan is present.

PROPHECIES IN THE BOOK OF ESTHER

Bibliography

Bytwerk, R. L. (2008). *Landmark Speeches of National Socialism.* College Station: Texas A&M University Press.

Cohen, A. A. (2009). *20th Century Jewish Religious Thought: Original Essays on Critical Concepts, Movements, and Beliefs.*, Philadelphia; Jewish Publication Society of America, . Philadelphia: Jewish Publication Society of America.

Culi, R. Y. (1979). *Me'am Lo'es - The Torah Anthology.* (R. A. Kaplan, Ed.) New York: Maznaim Publishing Corporation.

David Kanhowitz. (2001, March). Judaic Classics Libary. (2.2). Brooklyn, New York, USA.

Yechezkel, Artscroll Tanakh Series. (1977). (R. M. Eisemann, Trans.) Brooklyn, New York: Mesorah Publications.

Etheridge, J. W. (2017). *The Targums of Onkelos and Jonathan Ben Uzziel on the Pentateuch: With the Fragments of the Jerusalem Targum, From the Chaldee; Leviticus, Numbers and Deuteronomy.* London: Forgotten Books .

Fohrman, R. D. (2011). *The Queen You Thought You Knew; Unmasking Esther's Hidden Story.* USA, USA: OU Press in conjunctin with HFBS Publishing.

Ginzberg, L. (1987). *The Legends of The Jews.* Philadelphia : The Jewish Publication Society.

Hertz, D. J. (1948). *The Authorized Daily Prayer Book.* New York: Block Publishing.

Hertz, D. J. (1984). *Daily Prayer Book.* New York: Bloch Publishing Company.

Horowitz, E. (2006). *Reckless Rites: Purim and the Legacy of Jewish Violence*. Princeton: Princeton University Press.

Kadari, T. (2009, March 20). *Vashti: Midrash and Aggadah*. Retrieved December 27, 2017, from Jewish Women: A Comprehensive Historical Encyclopedia: https://jwa.org/encyclopedia/article/vashti-midrash-and-aggadah

Katz, D. M. (1996). *Computorah on Hidden Codes in the Torah* (Hebrew ed.). Jerusalem: Achdut Printing.

Layard, A. H. (1849). *Ninevah and Its Remains: A Narrative of an Expedition to Assyria*. London: John Murray.

Leitner, D. (2007). *Understanding the Alef-Beis: Insights Into the Hebrew Letters and the Methods for Interpretating Them*. Jerusalem, New York: Feldheim Publishers.

Munk, R. M. (1983). *The Wisdom in Hebrew Alphabet*. Brooklyn: Mesorah Publications.

Rabbi Nosson Scherman, R. M. (1981). *The Megillah - The Book of Esther*. Brooklyn, New York: Mesorah Publications, Ltd.

Robert Jamieson, A. R. (1999). *Jamieson, Fausset and Brown's Commentary*. Zondervan.

Rosenberg, R. A. (Ed.). (1982). *The Book of Isaiah - A New English Translation, Shorasim (a Rabbinic commentary)* (Vol. II). New York: The Judaica Press Inc.

Rubin, E. (2011, June 8). Purim 1946? Not Exactly. *Newsweek*, p. .

Sabua, R. B. (1992, August 1). The Hidden Hand of God. *Bible Review*, pp. 31-33.

Sacks, R. L. (2015). *The Koren Siddur* (Nusah Ashkenza, Lobel ed.). (R. L. Sacks, Trans.) Jerusalem, Israel: Koren Publishers.

Satrap. (2017, December 13). Retrieved December 27, 2017, from Wikipedia: https://en.wikipedia.org/wiki/Satrap

Schochet, E. J. (1991). *Amalek, The Enemy Within.* Los Angeles: Mimetav Press.

Singer, Isidore. (1907). *Jewish Encyclopedia Vol. 1-12.* (I. Singer, Ed.) New York, New York: Funk and Wagnalls Company.

Smith, K. (1946, October 16). Goering Ends Life in Cell; 10 Nazis Hang. *New York Daily News.*

Tokayer, M. D. (2011, January 21). *Yisro 5635 First Ma'amar.* Retrieved January 14, 2018, from sfasemes.blogspot.com: sfasemes.blogspot.com/search?q=Yisro

Walton, J. H. (1978). *Chronological And Background Charts of the Old Testament.* Grand Rapids: Zondervan.

Wikimedia Commons Contributors. (2017, July 27). *File:JudeanImpalement Roaf185.jpg,* ID: 253291001. Retrieved January 1, 2018, from Wikimedia Commons, the free media repository: https://commons.wikimedia.org/w/index.php?title=File:JudeanImpalement_Roaf185.jpg&oldid=253291001.

Wistrich, R. (1995, October 16). *Who's Who In Nazi Germany.* New York : Routledge.

Zlotowitz, R. M. (1976). *The Megillah.* Brooklyn: Mesorah Publications Ltd.

Rosh HaShanah and the Messianic Kingdom to Come

To understand the plan of mankind's restoration, one needs to look into the Holy Days as given by G-d. Each Holy Day explains a part of the divine plan of redemption. In his book, Good focuses on the latter days, specifically the fall festivals, as related to the second coming of Yeshua haMashiach (Yeshua the Messiah). Rosh Hashanah, also known as Yom Teruah (Day of Trumpets), is the start of these.

Good elegantly expresses the ancient beliefs of the Jewish people into an easy to understand narrative of the last days. He takes great care to support each subject with scriptural references.

Verse by verse, with insights gleaned from earlier writings, a clear picture starts to emerge of events leading up to the Messiah's return. Each chapter builds on the last leading up to the Messiah's coronation and wedding. The reader will travel an ancient path of Biblical knowledge that few students of the Bible ever see, learning the meanings behind Rosh HaShanah, the Days of Awe, Yom Kippur and Sukkot as defined by the Bible.

In his book, Joseph Good conveys the scriptures in a refreshing and beautiful way showing the Creator's love for His people. Encouraging, careful with details and above all, letting the Word speak its own message, *Rosh HaShanah and the Messianic Kingdom to Come* will encourage and sustain the reader as the return of the Messiah draws nearer.

This 4th edition has been revised and updated with additional materials.

Joseph Good can also be found on his weekly channel sponsored through his Hatikva Ministries. He is available for speaking engagements. For additional materials by the author including books, DVD's, and CD's, please visit -

www.hatikva.org

NOTES

NOTES

NOTES

ISBN-10: 1983915408

ISBN-13: 978-1983915406

Made in the USA
Coppell, TX
27 February 2025

46480490R00083